"The soul cannot be confined within
man-made boundaries.
Its nationality is Spirit;
its country is Omnipresence."

Paramahansa Yogananda

BRIGITTE SCHULZE

Sasha, pour one more!
With love and vodka through 25 years in Ukraine

pili edition

The Author

Brigitte Schulze was professionally active in Ukraine for more than twenty-five years. She began in Kiev as a freelance correspondent for numerous German media. Then, as a consultant for media policies, she promoted the professional development of journalists in Ukraine. In Odessa, she served several years as an advisor for cultural promotion and tourism. For her dedicated commitment to the presentation of an authentic picture of Ukraine to the rest of the world, in her travel guides and other publications, the Council for Tourism and Health Resorts in Kiev awarded her the title of *Ambassador for Ukrainian Tourism*. Repeatedly in the past, she had plans to leave Ukraine but a new, interesting project always detained her. When the conflict in East Ukraine began, she was in action again, this time as an observer with the Organization for Security and Cooperation in Europe (OSCE). Her precise observations and, in particular, her numerous personal contacts with the people in Ukraine give her a profound understanding of the country. In her travel books she describes her encounters with the Ukrainian people and country with sensitivity and empathy. Now, in this book, she presents a very personal view of her life and experiences in Ukraine. She intensively experienced the development of Ukraine during the years before and since independence in 1991. This makes her anecdotes and reports about this country so authentic.

Translation of the German edition
„Sascha, schenk' ein! Mit Liebe und Wodka durch 25 Jahre Ukraine"
Published in Germany 2016
ISBN 978-3-9814225-5-9, Paperback
ISBN 978-3-9814225-9-7, ebook

English translation published by pili edition in the US in 2017
ISBN 978-0-9995024-0-2, Paperback
ISBN 978-0-9995024-1-9, ebook
www.pili-edition.com

Copyright © Brigitte Schulze
www.brigitteschulze.de

Brigitte Schulze

Sasha, pour one more!

With love and vodka through 25 years in Ukraine

pili edition

The Book

It was a balancing act between two worlds – the safe, secure life in Germany on the one hand and the magical attraction of a foreign country on the other. With time, for the journalist and author, Brigitte Schulze, Ukraine became a second home. She lived and worked there for more than twenty-five years.

Kiev, Odessa, Kharkiv, Lviv, Dnipropetrovsk were some of the stations of her life in Ukraine – a life that was not always without personal risks. Courageously she met all challenges and implemented professional projects together with partners from Germany, Ukraine, and the countries of the European Union as well as of the United States.

When the war in East Ukraine began, she was appointed as an observer for the "Organization for Security and Cooperation in Europe" (OSCE).

Then came the first thoughts of leaving her beloved Ukraine. What had happened? What was the last straw? With her Ukrainian friends she found warmth and support but the social and bureaucratic structures of the country wore her continually down. Corruption and resentment had replaced the ideal of a common prosperity. At the same time, she had to see the people in eastern Ukraine suffer the effects of a dramatic conflict. The hope to bring about peace could not be realized.

The story contained in this book can be read like a novel. But it is the true story of the German author Brigitte Schulze who's life is full of every new adventures.

contents

Sasha, pour one more!. 11

The Beginning 23

Tender Love. 31

The Correspondent Years. 37

To Kiev by car 79

My Band and I 85

Freedom of the press 95

Odessa. 99

My greatest self-experiment 111

The Euromaidan. .117

Mission with the OSCE 125

The last sip of vodka. 137

A warm fur is important in Eastern Europe

Sasha, pour one more!

For the third time, Sasha pours a vodka. No, wait, Valera, the neighbor is also here. Today he's doing the honors. At least three times is mandatory. After that, no one counts anymore. We are drinking – a mixture of vodka and beer. Actually, that's not done in Ukraine. But that's what I feel like today. First of all, I'm thirsty; and second, I'm sad. Occasionally tears roll down my cheeks, like little pearls. It doesn't matter, I add some vodka. I have to get through this. But what has happened? Actually, nothing in particular. That's the whole problem, that nothing happens. I come to Kiev and don't know why. Or the original reasons have evaporated – the business with the books, the consulting services, the position as advisor. Don't I belong here any more, here where I lived and worked over twenty years? Have I stayed too long? Does Ukraine still need me? Did it ever need me? Or did I need it? Did I use it to earn money, first as a journalist, as a foreign correspondent, then as a media consultant, followed by a time in the crazy city of Odessa as an advisor for culture and tourism? No one sent for me. I wanted it myself. I planned it myself. I stumbled into the trap myself. I spun my own net, from which it seems I can no longer free myself. Or was there an inner calling? A voice that lured me to Kiev? What in the world did I want there? Back then in 1988, two years after the disaster in Chernobyl. Sasha says that it was exactly 25 years ago. He knows because his grandson, Anton, had just been born. Today, his daughter and son-in-law and the two grandchildren live in the USA. Zina, his wife, is there on a visit just now. That's right, back then I brought along Penaten cream, baby care products, and toys from Germany.

"Sasha, pour one more! I'm sad." My old friend does as I requested, sad himself because he knows that he can't really help me. How often did we have discussions about Ukraine, its history, its culture, the Ukrainian language, the politics – either in agreement or controversially? How often did I think I knew better, did I try to convince him that things could be done with Ukraine and its people? At home, a running battle was often waged between Sasha and Zina, his wife. She is from Murmansk, and therefore a Russian; he is Ukrainian. So they argued about which were the better people. Sometimes I thought they were really serious. But then they laughed again. No, their verbal mock battles were just daily banter.

Did I want to conquer a foreign part of the world? And why did it necessarily have to be Ukraine? Just because I had studied Russian at the university? Just because as a child I had seen Saint Basil's Cathedral in the Red Square on television and then absolutely wanted to go to the place where that impressive building stands? Is that all? Or is it because I also loved secret writing as a child and was delighted when no one could read the mirror writing I had come up with and even less the Cyrillic letters, later? Yes, I have always been attracted to mysteries, to those things that can't be easily understood. For me, the entire Soviet Union was a big mystery – and, incidentally, the entire Slavic sphere, until the present day. The more time I spend in Ukraine and send out my feelers from there – earlier I was often also in Russia – the more I notice that I can't reach my goal. There is always a boundary somewhere. The solution to the mystery is elsewhere. Maybe within me? There are only individual people in Ukraine to whom I feel really close, with whom my soul resonates. Their number grew over the course of the years. Do I really have to travel more than two thousand kilometers to Kiev in order to understand my own feelings? Couldn't I have done that cheaper at home in Frankfurt or in Weilheim? Apparently not.

The potatoes on my plate have all been eaten. I'm starving. I haven't eaten anything all day. "Sasha, make more!" I peel the potatoes that I brought myself. It has to be potatoes, real, big, beautiful Ukrainian potatoes, from Ukrainian earth. Four or five more, thinly sliced, then placed raw in the frying pan. They cook quickly, with lots of oil. I add some of the good Ukrainian mayonnaise to my plate. Today there has to be a lot of fat – real Ukrainian style. I want it like that. Occasionally a bite of herring. And, of course, more vodka. "Sasha, pour one more! I'm sad. I have to wash something down." I know that the vodka doesn't improve anything; it just lets the nagging thoughts temporarily slip into the background. Things will continue tomorrow. The problem or the situation will still be there.

That's right, 25 years ago Sasha's grandson, Anton, was born. Only a handful of cars were driving along the Khreshchatyk in Kiev. Ukraine was part of the large Soviet Union and I was right in the middle. I hardly realized what was happening as I began talking with Zina on the street and she immediately invited me to her home. I had just asked for the way to the Philharmonic. From this meeting grew a friendship, almost like family. At the time I was slightly older than thirty and Sasha and Zina were around ten years older. Today Sasha is over seventy. He sees poorly. He can no longer meet me at the metro station on the outskirts of Kiev, where they live, especially not in the snow of the century, in March 2013. But I know the way, even though the faceless prefabricated apartment buildings always irritate me. They all look the same. Sasha is standing in his slippers outside the door, next to the snow, waiting for me. We ride the jolting, dark, cramped elevator up to the sixth floor. We step out of the elevator and onto the small landing, onto which two apartments open. We enter Sasha's apartment, take off our boots, coat, and jacket, and make ourselves comfortable. I feel at home here. I use the toilet, wash my hands, and "Sasha, pour a drink!" Slowly I start to explain what has happened. Nothing much,

Snow and more snow

really. But the representatives of Munich Airport who, like me, were at the tourism trade fair in Kiev, have explained to me that Ukraine International Airlines (UIA), with whom they cooperate, don't want to buy my books, which I had offered especially for the launch of this airline's new flight from Munich to Kiev in June 2013. A perfectly normal business matter – a perfectly normal offer and a perfectly normal rejection. But what were the reasons? Why this decision? My books were not slick enough. They showed Ukraine too much as it really is, without enough cosmetic treatment. And that's what they said to me – to me who invested so much passion in the books. To me, who is being so honest, because that is exactly what readers like. I'm shocked. On the one hand, because of the financial aspect of the rejection and, on the other, because of

the lack of appreciation. Who makes such a decision anyway? Some young thing who has just become the manager for marketing and communications for the Ukrainian airline? It's always the same. You can't do business with the Ukrainians. Things progress only sluggishly or stagnate. I feel like I've been repelled. And it's not the first time. Why? In 2007, my job as advisor for culture and tourism came to an end. OK, a little break was a good idea. Financially there were no problems. And I was very hopeful that my book about Ukraine and the other books, about Lviv in West Ukraine and about Odessa, would get off to a good start. Especially during the 2012 UEFA European Football Championship, with games in four Ukrainian towns, when thousands of fans would be coming. Then came the bad press about Ukraine in Germany. Hardly any mention was made of the people. I suffered when I read the inaccurate, in my impression, reports of colleagues. Of course that had a negative impact on the sales of my books. The sales are too low. As a visiting card they are too expensive. And Ukraine is a kind of forgotten land, with no face and no image – or with a bad image. It's so difficult to fight against this with my writing, even though I still have so many good ideas. What should I do? What's going to happen?
Ukraine help me! I mean well. I want to help you get a face, an image that is worth seeing. Kiev, open yourself. You green city where I fell in love more than twenty years ago. A love that supported me and kept me busy for a long time.

"Sasha, pour one more!" The story can't be over yet, can it? I'm sad. What more has to happen to convince me to give up on Ukraine? Or should I buy myself a grave here? Am I digging it myself, like the young fellows that I saw today who were digging holes for new chestnut trees along Khreshchatyk street, surrounded by the snow of the century? While I was walking there it almost seemed as though Kiev has passed me by, or is in the process of passing me by. The people who are walking there keep getting younger. What do they know about the old Ukraine? For them, everything new is normal –the advertising, the goods in the numerous shops. That's just the way it is. Why would they care what it was like yesterday? Why would they be interested in hearing that I used to bring cheese from Germany to Kiev, sealed in plastic in my suitcase,

Digging holes for new trees

because either no Gouda was available in Kiev or I didn't want to have to wait in line for it. The taxi driver agreed: Yes, his son just turned thirty. For him, his father's problems were irrelevant. Ukraine will surely develop. The son doesn't know how things used to be.

In the epic snow, taking a taxi is also torture. Because none come. I ordered one the evening before, to drive to the tourism trade fair at 9:30 the following morning. At 8:30 that morning, the taxi company confirmed the order. At 9:30 the company phones to tell me there is no taxi in my vicinity. I phone the next company and get the same answer. This is repeated two more times. Then, finally, after I had decided to ride the metro, I get a call. There is a car for me. I go out, down to the corner, so that the driver won't have to drive up the street, through the snow which hasn't been cleared away. He explains to me that following the financial crisis in 2007, the taxi companies consolidated. Now there are approximately forty directors and one headquarters. There the requests are only received and then forwarded to the taxi drivers. Each driver receives, for example, between one hundred and thirty or one hundred and fifty such calls per day. And each driver decides himself which tour he wants to accept, which matches his location well or if he even wants to drive at all. In the past, all the taxis in each parts of the city waited in a line until they were assigned a fare. Today – it's chaos. Of course, in summer it's better. But in every Ukrainian city bad weather immediately has a detrimental affect on taxis and traffic. "Sasha, pour one more!" I'm sad. I want to drown my tears in vodka.

At the tourism trade fair, the minister for Crimean culture and tourism* greets me with the words, "We don't pay money." My lovingly designed, beautiful flyers are lying around. No one is bothering with them, no one is interested in them. Of course, I planned the trade fair. I was supposed to have my own booth. Then I could have been really present. But the supposed partners got sick and didn't send a replacement. And always just be an onlooker? No thank you. I'm tired of fighting with Ukrainian agencies and officials, so-called partners who are nothing of the kind. Tired of walking, of crossing streets, tired of hauling my weighty bag, in which I always carry a camera and recorder, writing things, extra batteries, my books to show, a few brochures, more or less heavy. When the bag is full it surely weighs between fifteen and twenty pounds. Is it just age or is it the result of a lack of appreciation, or really a lack of love? Did there used to be more appreciation in the past? In the past there was generally more enthusiasm for the Ukraine. There was the ambassador, or actually a series of ambassadors who highly valued the freedom of the press, who had an affinity for the media. Establishing the seminars for journalists was easy. And then a job for me even materialized. Although I did always have to fight. It was a job that had to be renewed every three months until the structures were changed and I received a

---

* The Crimean Peninsula was annexed by Russia in March 2014.

year's contract. No one can avoid it. In one form or the other they are all inmates of a structural prison, hampered by rules, personal preferences, interests, and the work of the various lobbyists. Do I want to go back into that prison? Haven't I grown out of it? Isn't it something else that I want? To show "my" Ukraine, "my" people, who are such good people? Not divided into East and West but into the helpful ones with their open hearts and those who take advantage of the need of their fellow man for their own profit. Like the taxi driver who used the snow chaos as a reason to charge eighty hryvnya (approximately eight euros)* for the short ride, instead of the standard twenty (approx. two euros), which it costs during good weather. And then there are the good people, who set their own Jeeps in motion, mobilize friends through Facebook, pack thermos bottles full of hot tea, and help others free themselves from the masses of snow, under which entire villages were buried. These were the people who made the "Orange Revolution" possible, the peaceful demonstrations which followed the presidential elections in 2004. The supporters of the unsuccessful candidate, Viktor Yushchenko, whose campaign color was orange, accused the opposite side of electoral fraud. They took to the streets and protested. They all helped one another, with meals, coffee, tea, and especially with moral support. Maybe that is what it is. A large portion of deep spirituality, which I have always felt in Ukraine. People who are humane and are not just functioning. And maybe that is why I am (still) there.

* Exchange rate 2013

Do I have to stay? Do I want to stay? Haven't I realized that the secret lies inside myself? Do I have to keep moving, keep traveling? I don't know. "Sasha, pour one more!" In any case, I have to write about it all. Maybe that will help to solve the mystery.

Gradually feeling at home in Kiev

The Beginning

Kiev 1988. I am traveling to Ukraine for the first time, to participate in a language course. It is crucial that I brush up on the Russian which I had learned at one time. After all, I want to reach my goal of seeing Moscow, the Red Square, and Saint Basil's Cathedral. A festival is being planned by Germany – nine months of contemporary music in the former Soviet Union. And I want to participate – as a reporter. To do that, I must speak Russian better. It's been a long time since I took my final examination at the university in Giessen, Germany. So I register at Shevchenko University in Kiev.

I had entirely forgotten. Since it was 1988, it was only two years after the explosion of the atomic reactor in Chernobyl. That fact didn't occur to me until my friends and acquaintances in Germany mentioned it. Wasn't I afraid to travel to Kiev? Wouldn't I change my plans? But I was already registered. And I had already paid. In my head everything was spinning. What is the situation with the radiation? Is it still dangerous there? How much is Kiev affected? For a week I racked my brain. I didn't want my dreams to be destroyed.

Finally, I took off – to a radiant Kiev in August.
With the train I travel from Berlin, via Brest in Belarus, to Kiev. When I arrive there, I move into university

housing. I am full of drive and enthusiasm. No airs and graces, no fears, just curious expectations. But even with this basic attitude, I find that the situation takes some getting used to. The student housing is not the least bit cozy and also not particularly clean. I don't really remember much about the sanitary facilities. Everything is beautifully dreadful. But at that time I didn't have enough money to find better – and therefore more expensive – living quarters. I had to accept the situation as it was. And it was more or less okay. The group was cheerful and I was learning Russian, more or less well.

The city itself shows no traces of Chernobyl. Kiev is as green and beautiful as ever, in summer. As far as the people are concerned, I can't find anything which points to the catastrophe in Chernobyl. I am told that their nails grew faster. This summer, and also in the following years, the school holidays have been extended to make it possible for the children to thoroughly recuperate in the countryside, far from Chernobyl. Every day, the streets and buildings are sprayed with water. Is this intended to wash away the radio activity?

The Russian classes at the university took their course, more or less. I wasn't really satisfied with them. I wanted to speak the way it is spoken every day life. That didn't really happen until I got acquainted with a group of young men. It was there that I slowly began to learn colloquial Russian.

Here's the way it was in those days, in the Soviet Union: You just got passed from one social contact to the other. If you became part of a network, then you would never be lost again. A German woman from the church, with whom I had come into contact through various other contacts, had given me the address and telephone number of the young tour guide, Dima. She was incredibly enthusiastic about the boat trip, south on the Dnepr (in Ukrainian, it's called the Dnipro), and about the young people she had met on the boat. That's why I wasn't at all worried. I thought, that if the church is involved, nothing can go wrong. I just phoned Dima. And from that point on, things happened almost automatically. He invited me to join this group. So there we sat, in the lobby of the mediocre Soviet hotel, Mir, in Kiev, and tried to talk to one another. Oh, was that difficult then! And sure, in those days, it didn't take long before one was invited to an apartment. Pubs or restaurants – that wasn't common. There were hardly any of them, and the few there were, were unpleasant and expensive.

I could feel my heart beating as I walked with Dima along the dark streets of Kiev, into the dark stairwell, up the stairs, and then into the apartment. At first I was frightened. What was I getting involved with here? Was it necessary to always know everything? The apartment door opened – and there were only young men, five or six or seven. A group of friends. Oh no, not that. Not a single woman. But then I was inside. And it wasn't so bad after all. One of the young men began cooking. There were noodles for dinner, if I remember correctly. And vodka, of course. And some kind of sauce with the noodles. The dark young man from the south – an Armenian as I learned later – had made the sauce. We talked as well as we could, in Russian. I studied all of them – Dima, Edik, and the others. In Edik's eyes, especially, I found something that fascinated me. So much trust, so much warmth, so much openness. "I'm married," he said right away. "But I have a friend who is free." But I hadn't said anything. Was it so easy to see my need for closeness and attention? I was impressed, impressed that I had inadvertently stumbled into a group of humanists.

The next day Sergey had joined the group. I liked him right away. After one of the next get-togethers, we went for a walk together, through Kiev's numerous parks. The night was warm. We talked. He explained much to me about the Soviet Union of those days. I was sad. I had seen how the people lived; what could be bought in the shops, and what could not; how long the lines were when chickens or tomatoes had just become available again. Svetlana, Sergey's mother, who I would get to know later and who was to become a close friend, had a huge bowl of tomatoes in the kitchen. I estimated it to be at least forty pounds of tomatoes. Some were still green but many were red – and after a while they became moldy because they couldn't be used up fast enough. I asked one question after the other and always received patient answers. I still didn't understand the life there. But that didn't matter – I wanted the experience. Count me in.

Edik, from the group, looked at me sympathetically. No, it wasn't really all that bad there. And, besides, I couldn't carry all the weight on my narrow shoulders. But that's what I wanted to do. Become president of the Soviet Union and do everything differently so that the people there would be better off. Delusions of grandeur? Little revolutionary, as my mother sometimes called me? I don't know. I was sad because I could do so little to help. The young men laughed about it. And I understood that least of all. At some point, I left the country again. Then I spent some time in New York and a year later, I was back in the Soviet Union. It was 1990. I was in my mid-thirties. Contemporary German Music in the Soviet Union, a music festival organized by the German Music Council, began. I was there, as the music critic for the newspaper *Frankfurter Allgemeine Zeitung*. I traveled to Moscow for the opening, to Leningrad, that today is again called St. Petersburg, to Kemerovo in Siberia, and to Barnaul. Everywhere concerts of modern music, with German musicians, took place. And then it was Kiev's turn to host a few events. So I returned. Sergey and I had corresponded in the meantime – pen pals. Sometimes he even phoned me. That must have been horrendously expensive, considering his circumstances. I felt honored. The nice man from Kiev was phoning me. But I wasn't really sure what I should talk to him about. One thing was certain, however. The many letters, back and forth, helped my Russian improve continually.

When, a few months later, he invited me to visit him in Kiev, I simply accepted the invitation. I bought a ticket. It was winter – February or March – and bitterly cold in Kiev. I arrived wearing the fur coat which I had bought especially for the trips to Eastern Europe. Sergey picked me up from the airport, in a huge bus belonging to the Intourist travel organization, for which he was working at the time. I remember everything exactly. How we tramped through the snow. He with my heavy suitcase, followed by me in my broad-shouldered fur coat. His mother, Svetlana, saw us from the window and disappeared discreetly. A meal had been cooked and was waiting on the stove in the kitchen. There was no turning back. So I immersed myself in Ukrainian life.

Carpets on the walls and brown, varnished furniture

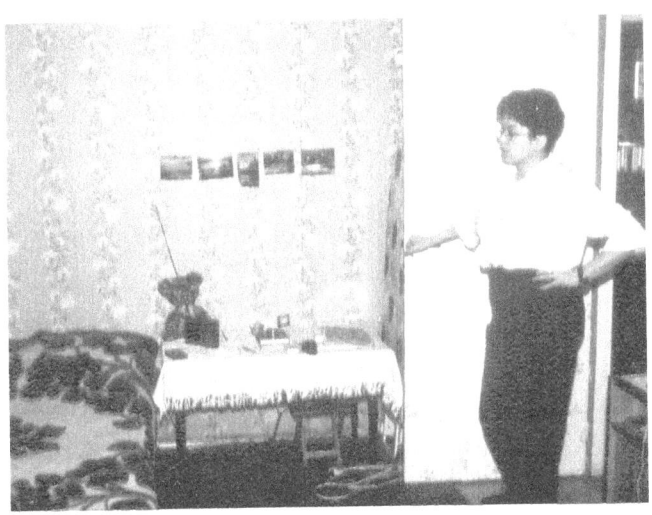

Doors covered with wall paper

I planted basil in an old flower box

Tender Love

The apartment: Brown varnished furniture, in the style of the Fifties, and the same hardwood flooring in all rooms. Shelves full of books, silver-colored curtains, and colorful rugs. One room was renovated and the other was a junk room, so much had been placed and stored in it. The toilette was calcified, yellowed and leaky. The water was constantly running. In the kitchen stood an old sofa. That's where we kissed for the first time, in the middle of the night, at 1:30, with vodka and cognac. I asked Sergey, who I learned to lovingly address with the diminutive form, Seryozha, what he wished for from life. In those days, the Soviet Union still existed and the people didn't wish for anything because the fulfillment of any possible wish was so hard to imagine. I didn't give up. "What do you wish for? What do you want to achieve in life?" No answer. Only a deep smile, that came from a long way away. Even then, that was incomprehensible to me. My philosophy was, that if a person has no goals, he can't achieve anything. But everything was different there.

And then it became a tender and deep love. And the first that taught me so much about life. About life in a country that is unpredictable, due to its possibilities and impossibilities. A love that showed me a part of life, from the core, from life's blazing center. We lived in "luxury". Two people in a two-room apartment, which his mother had left so we could be alone. The grandmother lived in the country and the brother and mother lived in a second apartment, on the outskirts of the city. On one of my next visits, we had to move together with the brother and I was disappointed. I wanted to have Seryozha all to myself again and I made a fuss until I understood what he was explaining to me. His mother had four more guests spending the night in her apartment. Today I have learned to crowd together with the people I love, to share a bed. The body needs 20 inches of space; the soul has already learned right where it belongs.

On the sofa in the kitchen we had night-long discussions about everything imaginable. I asked, was amazed, wanted to know everything about life in Ukraine. And Sergey answered with a smile. Once he said that real freedom could only be inside a person – very deep in the soul. I just couldn't imagine that. Freedom, that meant democracy, the openness of a country, the freedom to do – or not to do – what I wanted. In the Soviet Union everything was regulated and defined. How was it possible to find inner freedom in such a situation? That was a mystery to me. So I just left it at that. Then came another one of his ideas: A person could also love a beggar. Love wasn't a question of coming from the same social level. I couldn't understand that either. Love a beggar? Somehow it all confused me. But then there was always his smile, his charm, and his wonderful, true, tender, deep love.

The two week stay turned into more. Sergey's character was amazing. I invited him to Germany. We even wanted to get married. He wanted three children. I was in my prime. But then came the illness. Without warning; too much stress. A kind of burnout. I was sent to a course of health treatments. And the dream was over. I felt overwhelmed by the situation – to bring a man with no job and only minimal knowledge of German to Germany, to marry him, and provide for him. It was all I could do to take care of myself and support myself with my job as a freelance journalist. After a long inner struggle, I called off the plan. Even though he had already taken care of all the paperwork in Kiev.

For a long time I reproached myself and suffered from a sense of unfulfilled love. Again and again I wondered what it would have been like, if only …. The love for Seryozha had awakened and assured me. For me it was – yes, what was it? Definitely not just a tourist's love. Under no circumstances had I wanted that. I wanted to be able to look myself in the eye. But what my wishes were beyond that was not clear to me. Maybe I liked playing with fire? With a fire that can warm but that can also burn? That fire burned in me for more than twenty years and led me to see everything in Ukraine through loving eyes – sometimes against my better judgment. As a foreign correspondent, I reported with loving eyes. I was always looking for the best aspects and had to report about things that were not so good.

That often put me in a moral conflict with the rules of my profession.

The times have changed. Today, everyone in Ukraine wishes at least for a nice apartment, a car, a television, attractive clothing. And many can even afford this.

Later, when I occasionally saw Seryozha, I could feel my heart beating faster and faster. Even after the end of our relationship, I remained integrated in his family and his mother has remained a good friend, up to the present. He is married. His wife is nice, unremarkable. Whenever we met at the occasional family birthday celebration and talked to one another, it all came back to me. A wave of warmth flowed through me. But these meetings also came to an end. The pain was just too great, including that on the side of his wife who, of course, noticed everything. In addition, Seryozha withdrew into himself. When I saw him the last time, he seemed to have aged internally, as if his soul had been broken. His charm has evaporated, or at least he no longer shows it. He owns a car and drives it as a taxi at night, to earn money. He has a wife who provides for him, who works as an interpreter to bring money into the house. They have a dog and black Italian furniture. Later a daughter was born. The question about what he wished for from life – would I ask him that again today?

At the Kiev airport

The Correspondent Years

After several short research trips to Ukraine, in May 1993 I was accredited by the Ukrainian State Department as a permanent freelance correspondent, through the *Frankfurter Allgemeine Zeitung*. My parents were sad that I was so far away. After all, the distance between Frankfurt, where I was living at the time, and Kiev is roughly 2,500 kilometers. But they accepted the fact. They had also been sad three years earlier, in 1990, when I had announced that I was no longer a member of the Lutheran Church. After all, my father's father had been a Lutheran pastor and my great-grandfather had been general superintendent in the church. In addition, there were several deaconesses in the family. Up to the present day, the last four generations of my father's family have counted seven people who became pastors. I just wanted out of that clique; wanted to find my own way. Searching, always searching. In Ukraine I seemed to have found something, something in the people that I couldn't find in Germany. Closeness, warmth, security – voluntary and not forced.

How often have I pondered over the Ukrainian mentality? How often did I return to Frankfurt from Kiev, crying my eyes out? My parents and very close friends picked me up at the airport and helped pick me up emotionally, as well. Many times. At some point it became easier – or I got used to traveling between two worlds. When no one was available to pick me up, I increasingly had to deal with the impressions from Kiev on my own, without friends and family at my side. Somehow I accomplished it. But stress and strain on every trip have remained to the present day.

What is it which forces a person to leave their comfort zone and their own cultural area? For example, the journalist Tiziano Terzani, whom I admire, came to feel at home in Asia. Ultimately, he had also been searching for something in his life, like we all do – for a deeper sense, for something spiritual, for something which only reveals itself when things are tranquil. But for me there was no trace of tranquility. My life was entirely filled with impressions of the "new" country. I "fought" my way through the politics and economics of Ukraine and let myself be moved. I criticized and tried to research objective information.

The first years were difficult for me. In the beginning, culture and music were my main topics. After all, as a musicologist, these fields were dear to me and as a long-time music critic for the *Frankfurter Allgemeine Zeitung*, they were part of my job. On the other hand, the first twenty-minute business feature for the *Deutschlandfunk* (German radio station), for the *"Background"* (*"Hintergrund"*) series was a real challenge.

It was the period in which Leonid Kravchuk was the first president of a Ukraine which had received independence in 1991. His time in office lasted until 1994. Then Leonid Kuchma, from the training ground of East Ukraine, came into power. He remained president of Ukraine for almost eleven years. Once I flew in the Kuchma presidential plane from Munich to Kiev, together with the entire presidential staff of cabinet ministers, security men, and Ukrainian journalists. I was so proud to be included. Then, as now, everyone turned a blind eye and didn't ask about the skeletons in the closets of Ukrainian politicians. Sure, we knew where this president had come from, but Germany was glad to have the same contact person over a long period of time, someone whose behavior was more or less predictable and with whom a relationship could be established. Why could Kuchma remain so long in office? What happened to the Ukrainian journalist, Georgiy Gongadze, who was murdered on September 17th, 2000? At the time, those weren't issues yet. I simply wanted to do my work as well as possible. I wanted to be involved, to find good topics, to write interesting, understandable background reports, and to be appreciated as a correspondent.

My first apartment in Kiev was on Lipki street (Russian: ulitsa Lipki, Ukrainian: vulytsya Lypky), in the best part of town. Visits from the landlord were included. Once, when I had a cold, the landlord brought me medicine and even sat by my bedside. A total stranger. I was shocked. He had a key to the apartment. As soon as I could, I hunted for a new place. The new apartment was a few streets away, around the corner, in the lane Klosvkiy Spusk (transcribed from Ukrainian Klovskyj Uzviz). There, on the whole, I had my peace. Measuring a little less than 50 square meters, the two-room apartment was small but it was big enough to live in it and to begin setting up a correspondent's office. And most importantly, I was free from unwelcome contact with the landlord there.

Gradually I became acquainted with Ukrainian life in Kiev. Sometimes there was no hot water, and sometimes no water at all. If there was no hot water, I heated water on the gas stove, in a red enamel teakettle, poured it into a large white enamel bowl, added cold water, then used a large, 8 oz. cup to slowly pour the water over my head. Many times I "showered" like this, in Kiev and also later in Odessa. Why did I put up with it all? In Germany my life was more comfortable. But I was searching for something which I really couldn't define. The heart loves adventure. Of course, everyone has their own life plan. I have believed that for a long time. And my plan included venturing into the Slavic world. I wanted to become acquainted with the life

The kitchen

there in the East. And I wanted to find truth, a truth about life, there where it is elemental, and as I hadn't known it up until that time. At least, that's what it seemed to me then. In my attempt to look behind the scenes I often reached my own limits. There is no simple, common truth there where I found myself. Paradox reigns there. My relations with the people felt true. The effort to look behind the scenes, during my journalistic research, most often confronted me with the opposite.

After having followed a long path through the world, I increasingly find my truth here in Germany. Here where I was born, where I "enjoyed" my socialization, where "my" church is, where Jesus, Maria, and Joseph are, where spiritual teachers are found, and where my family originates. In other words, inside myself.

But back to Kiev, then, in the early Nineties, in the small apartment with the brown varnished furniture, in the brick building, called a Khrushchevka. This term goes back to the head of the Soviet government, Nikita Khrushchev, who was head of the CPSU from 1953 to 1964 and head of the government from 1958 to 1964 and who, in the '60s and '70s had such buildings built. Most of them had five stories. My apartment was on the second story, in the Ukrainian method of counting the floors of a building. In the hallway of the building, the light often doesn't work. The stairway is bare concrete and is always dirty. A different smell of

The living room/office

cooked food seeps out from under the door of each apartment. On the balcony, semi-transparent plastic is stretched along the railing. On the narrow sides, on the right and left, there are even two planters with old soil, in which, however, nothing is growing. In one year, I courageously sowed basil seeds in one of the planters. And they actually sprouted. Apparently the famous Ukrainian black earth lives up to its reputation. Just think what the agricultural industry could achieve here, with a little more expertise! I harvested basil all summer, up into October. All

The building entrance

my Ukrainian friends marveled at the green leaves. They didn't know what basil was. Many didn't even know lettuce. That was hardly available anywhere in Kiev at the time. Cabbage, on the other hand, could be found everywhere. Inna once said, "When people only have the bare minimum, they don't consider whether or not to plant a second type of lettuce."

The bathroom: Small, square, light blue tiles – chipped here and there – and with flowered wallpaper above. In the rooms, a few curtains hang from the ceiling, one with a green leaf pattern. The double windows are drafty. In autumn, as a precautionary measure, I brought adhesive foam strips from Germany, to seal the windows. When I affix them, I see that the foam strips don't even begin to close the cracks. It is still drafty.

I look out of the window of my apartment. One of the two rooms is a connecting room. On the other side of the street is a ten-story building that robs me of sunlight, from mid-day onward. On the little hill below I see people who are walking their dogs or carrying heavily loaded bags home. Everyone carries the bread in their hands, one loaf of white bread and one loaf of black bread. Trees grow outside all the windows of the apartment. In fact, all of Kiev is very green.

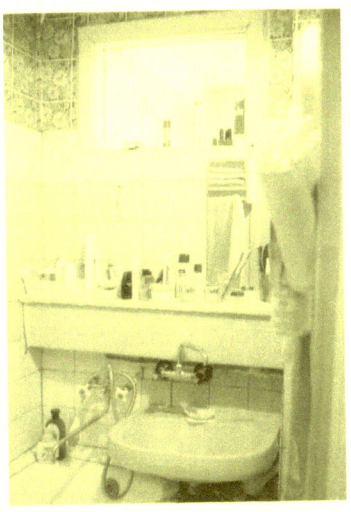

The bathroom

In summer, I feel like I am in a gigantic park here. But in autumn and winter, when the trees have lost their leaves and there is no snow to beautify everything with white, it looks dismal.

Outside my apartment two men are standing and drinking beer. I often see them there, sitting or standing and drinking. Sometimes they are drinking vodka. Once I even saw one of my musician colleagues from the Kiev brass band in which I played for several years. He was totally drunk. Even in winter they stand there, the men in their fur hats, with bottles in their hands. Later, when the bottles are empty, they just throw them into the bushes. A friend explained that the old women collect the bottles and turn them in for the deposit – a small additional source of income.

Once when I returned to Kiev after a two-month's absence in Germany, I was appalled. In the meantime, my landlady had painted the kitchen – light blue. I can't stand that color. But it's not so much the color as the fact that the blue paint had just been carelessly brushed over the original yellowed white. All the edges were smeared and the paint didn't even cover thoroughly. Some paint even ended up on the heater. After I installed a new lock in my door, I didn't have to worry about that happening again. The kitchen cupboard holds old dishes, cups with broken-off handles, and aluminum flatware that leaves an unpleasant taste when eating. And everywhere flowered wallpaper …

The landlady didn't allow me to paint white over the hideous dark brown of the varnished furniture, as I did in later apartments in Kiev and Odessa. That was always the first thing I did. Buy paint and primer, and sandpaper, and start painting. The result was always very good. I wanted to create a piece of the West in the East. And I constantly have to remind myself, "I am here of my own free will. No one sent me. I decided on this myself."

Then, first of all, I had to have a fax. I brought the machine from Germany. The connection was considerably more difficult. In those days there were no fax switches in Ukraine. The German cables didn't fit in the Ukrainian – or at the time, Soviet – sockets. So I had to bring everything along – telephone jacks, cables, plugs, small tools …. I tinkered around, by myself and with the help of others, to get the Ukrainian connection to work with German attachments. Finally it worked. But in those days the wires were tapped. Maybe they are today also, but it's just not as noticeable as it used to be. Then, a telephone conversation was simply over, at the most after twenty or twenty-five minutes. During a fax transmission there were also often interruptions, when I wanted to send pages of manuscripts to Germany, for reports or broadcasts. Most of the time I needed several attempts before I was successful. The follow-up action was to telephone, to hear if everything had arrived well.

A tricky fax Installation

For seven years I lived in this small apartment and from here I took my journalistic tours through Kiev and Ukraine. I was one of the first German journalists in Ukraine, following its independence in 1991. In addition to myself, there was one more permanent correspondent from the *Spiegel* news magazine. On the

My workstation

side of the German media, enthusiasm for reports on Ukraine was great. My articles, broadcasts and features about Ukraine sold very well. Everyone wanted to know something. My "vendor's tray", as the collection of various customers and contractors for freelance journalists is called, grew increasingly larger.

I was often asked where the information came from. Life brought it to me. I went out on the street and talked to friends and other people. I went to the foreign ministry, had meetings with authors, artists, musicians, and politicians. I accompanied German business people on their travels through the country. Everywhere I asked my way around and I went wherever I could. That was painstaking; much more difficult than it is today. First, I always had to convince the receptionist, the so-called *priyomniki* or *pomochniki* (helper), that I had to enter, for an interview. Giving information and sharing knowledge was not at all common during this time. People were still suffering from the conditions of the newly collapsed Soviet Union, where everyone spied on everyone else and where real information was only discussed secretly, at the kitchen table. When something did occasionally happen fast, I was immediately suspicious. Statements which were given at press conferences generally made me skeptical. I was much more interested in daily life. What was it like? And I always searched for people. I wanted to understand what they are like, what they think, why they are as they are, and not otherwise.

After all, that's why I came. And, finally, I have to dissolve the love, the love for Sergey, which I didn't live out and which I possibly even betrayed. I go on my way, hoping to find a little more with each new encounter. But sometimes I don't understand anything at all, neither Ukraine nor the people who live there. I am reminded of a report about my work as a foreign correspondent which I wrote for a journalist's journal in 1997. I could have just as well written it today:

WITHOUT SAFETY NET AND DOUBLE BOTTOM – MOMENTS IN THE LIFE OF A CORRESPONDENT*

I see them all coming and going – the ambassadors, the embassy staff, the ARD (Consortium of public broadcasters in Germany) correspondents, the company representatives. And I remain. In any case, I was one of the first German correspondents to get permanent accreditation in Ukraine. At that time hardly anyone yet thought that Ukraine could be seen differently than through the Moscow-tinted glasses of the journalists who had been accredited in Russia. And to this very day, broadcasters and editors who are in charge at the large print media will refer one to the existence of their Moscow office for questions about Ukraine, mostly due to laziness and ignorance. Up to today, Ukraine is officially included in the news coverage area of the CIS, which is handled from Moscow and in which no other journalist is allowed to "poach". The editorial team of the ARD bureau in Moscow is also in agreement

* Published July 1997 in "Sage und Schreibe"

here. The fact that this position sometimes leads to the distribution of anti-Ukrainian reports, which are based on the partially fabricated or only limited truths of the Russian news agencies, is (un)consciously accepted.
This makes it even more difficult for a German journalist to write against ignorance and lack of knowledge and to inform people about Ukraine. It is the result of my marketing technique that the cash register rings, despite this situation. But the hawking at the doors of German editorial offices involves much toil and tribulation – the daily mailing of offers, to the ARD, the daily newspapers, and professional journals; the daily need to find new topics or to present existing topics in a new context; the daily search for new clients and the task of convincing people of the increasing importance of Ukraine in European foreign affairs. A reference to a hardship allowance in addition to the standard remuneration is generally ignored. In times when everyone is on short rations, people are happy to shirk the responsibility for the payment of research and travel fees. I work under the most primitive conditions and live in Kiev in a two-room apartment under local conditions. Carpets hang on the walls of my apartment. Ants are permanent visitors to kitchen and bath. The furniture, in the style of the Fifties, is threadbare. My only tie to the West is through fax and telephone – and that only when I am victorious over the poor connections.
Had I ever stood in line was the question that Yura, my Ukrainian journalist colleague once asked me. Yes, of course, and I also felt the aggression begin growing in

me. Why wait in such a line? Why does it even exist? What kind of people are they who patiently get in line and wait for hours for the opening of some office, business or whatever? People who have learned to wait? People who patiently accept everything? I'm not like that. I always want everything, and right now. I have to learn something here; a part of life that is different than all I knew before. It's difficult for me to put it into words. Reports about Ukraine – factual information? How can that be possible here, where everything is shaped by personal stories. Politics – there too, people are at work, with their very personal stories, their wishes and dreams, because of which they often and easily become involved in power struggles. Being human – that means life. And life changes every day, as does each person, in each new situation. You lose a bit and gain a bit. That's the way it is in this country also and it's only with difficulty that it can be described with words and sentences. But I attempt it just the same; try to illuminate Ukraine from my own personal viewpoint, with all five senses, as a journalist ....

I began with the Ukrainian friends from my time at the university in Kiev. Without these social contacts, access to this country – then still the Ukrainian Soviet Republic – would have been impossible. The family with which I lived for a long period, crowded closer together in their cramped living quarters and helped me get my bearings, when I didn't yet have a Ukrainian press card from the foreign ministry.

My daily life in Kiev is characterized by running around, lugging bags with the most basic purchases, making appointments, and appearing everywhere personally because that's the only way to reach a goal, if at all. Research. Where to begin? How to end? My articles and broadcasts which I write for the Frankfurter Allgemeine Zeitung, *professional journals, and the ARD's TV stations remain fragments. They seem to me to be only temporary snapshots and they are, of course, shaped by my Western intellect. It often leads me astray and thereby also leads my Western logic ad absurdum. The one thing which unites my impressions is the continual unpredictability, the unforeseeability. Against all the rules, this can sometimes even have a positive effect. I comfort myself with this in moments of frustration – when the telephone doesn't function, when appointments are broken, when ministers aren't available, when statistics are outdated or manipulated. In any case, information becomes obsolete faster than it can be printed, broadcast, or published. Whom can I believe? It's best to believe no one. I only believe that which I see, hear, or feel, in other words, that which I experience myself. Everything takes at least twice as long as it does elsewhere and when it does occasionally go fast, I'm suspicious. Naturally, when Ukraine was on the brink of being accepted to the Council of Europe (November 9, 1995), I was offered an interview with the speaker of parliament, Aleksander Moroz. But I am still waiting for an interview with the minister of defense or with the president, Leonid Kuchma. Official information is often withheld. Often, I feel hindered in my work by agencies and ministries. The dealings with Western journalists are still clumsy and awkward, and not only in the press office of the president.*

My path is difficult – and maybe therefore also more interesting? I live at the grassroots, among the people, and experience everything from below. Sometimes I experience discomfort when I climb through the dark, dirty entryway to my Kiev apartment. But, nevertheless, I have felt safe and at home there for almost the last five years. Radio Ukraine supported me with my work. There I occasionally produce my reports for the German broadcasters. In Ukraine, no one is in charge of agreements on international program exchanges. Everyone wants and needs to earn money. So I pay for the "friendship" in the studio. However, over the years, interpersonal chemistry has developed. I live together with these people and I accept them – that's part of it all. Otherwise I wouldn't get anywhere, especially not in my status as a freelance colleague.

Sometimes I begin work out of the blue, when I run into interesting people and situations. For topics such as "Chernobyl" I have to live with the competition of colleagues from stations and newspapers who have a larger budget at their disposal, who can afford photographers, camera teams, travel expenses, hotels, and the customary favor payments which facilitate and accelerate many a contact. In Ukraine, more than elsewhere, a journalist must also earn a certain trust from dialogue partners. It is seldom that someone willingly agrees to an interview during a first contact. And when it does happen, it is often a sign that probably no usable information will be received from this person. It is best to cancel right away; that saves times and nerves. I am already aware of this. I know how to deal with the people that I contact.

Still, I'm pondering whether I should stay and continue my work or break camp and leave. How much strength do I have left, with no budget and just good ideas? What's my résumé of many years of contact with Ukraine and five of which as an accredited correspondent? Now things can finally get going, with my experiences, with the infrastructure that I have created, and with a Ukrainian press card for two more years in my hand ....

When I read these lines, it seems to me as though time has stood still. And the text had already appeared in the journalist's periodical, *Sage und Schreibe* in 1997. Why was it always Ukraine, time and again? Why time and again pain and worry but also so much vitality? For example, on the weekend trips to Oleg's dacha. I enjoyed them especially. Oleg's dacha was beautiful, planted with flowers, while the neighbors had only planted potatoes and other edibles. In the evenings we made a campfire, roasted shashlik (in Russian, you say shashliki, with the emphasis on the last i), and drank vodka. And sometimes we then went swimming in the nearby stream, in the middle of the night.

On the other hand, the toilet culture – or lack of it – is a vexing topic. It doesn't exist – at least it didn't then. I was always on the lookout for a toilet brush and somewhat softer toilet paper. But in those days, these accoutrements couldn't be found anywhere or only after much searching. The same was true for a plastic bowl.

Instead there was gray writing paper. I have already searched unsuccessfully through ten stores for these items. "But you don't want to eat out of the toilet," one of my best friends once said to me. But still ... I want to clean the toilet, wash the windows, and feel a little "German" in this country which is so unfamiliar to me but which I have begun to love, despite all the gloomy predictions and despite the fact that everything here is so different and the socialist scent, as I call it, envelopes everything – a mixture of bad gasoline, mothballs, strong tobacco, human body odor, and perfume.

This text also flowed from my pen at the end of the Nineties, for a brochure to accompany an exhibit on the explosion in the power plant at Chernobyl, which I had organized. I realize that I have unexpectedly invested more than twenty years in the adventure called Ukraine. I don't know why. Is it only because of the money that I earn(ed)? No! Ukraine was always more for me than just a "work place". I really entwined myself with the life there. I feel like a part of it, but still remain on the outside. To the present day, I am hunting for explanations and answers to things that I don't understand. Did or do other correspondents feel the same way? In all the years, and up to the present day, I felt/feel as though I am caught in a jar of honey, from which no escape is possible, stuck in the inscrutable relationships of Ukrainian daily life. Often I have the feeling that something is being kept from me, that it is being kept secret. It's not the salient occurrences but the subtle nuances. It is extremely difficult to find one's way in the jungle of spoken and unspoken rules and the web of relationships.

What is this subtle something which seems to lurk behind an invisible curtain, ready to strike when I least expect it? After all, the people in Ukraine eat and drink just as you and I do. They laugh and love as you and I do. They work and strive for recognition as you and I do. They wish for prosperity, health, and luck, just as you and I do.

But they slide commercial documents into transparent covers, from the bottom. They often come too late – or not at all – without an excuse. In the echelons of political power they thwart themselves. They don't trust the quality of their own work. That's why pipes and wiring are laid above ground and on top of plaster. They are easier to repair that way. People can sometimes be malicious and do damage, like one of my landladies. During my absence, she turned on the water in the bathroom, to deliberately make me liable for a renovation of the apartment. I got off lightly. My girlfriend noticed it in time and turned off the water. The standard bathroom threshold – non-existent in Germany – prevented any great harm. They often behave illogically, as, for example, in the case of Lyudmila. She arranged for the cellar of the house where she lives to be cleaned out. Eight truckloads of rubble and rubbish are carted off. Someone complained. A letter arrived from the municipal building management. This activity had not been authorized. Everything must be returned to the original state. Otherwise she has to pay a fine. So the rubbish has to be returned? Or: I plan to have a balcony built onto my apartment in Odessa. The legal permit for this is not issued for a long time, despite high "fees", so I begin construction without the permit. One day a letter arrives in which the building authority announces that the balcony could not be approved, because it already existed. They are also occasionally crafty and trip themselves up, like the policemen who inadvertently flagged down their boss on the street when he drove by in the large car of a friend. He laughed at them. Ha ha – you tried to get money from the wrong guy. The boss made the policemen buy him 20 liters of gas at the next gas station. They don't know what image means and don't understand how much of it they lose, in respect to the Western world.

But still ... they are hospitable. They are helpful. They are intelligent. They are talented. They are well educated. They are clever. They are loving. What is not to understand? A young Russian woman who lives in Germany, helps me out. Russians and Ukrainians – the Slavs in general – are simply jealous of the life of those in the West. For one thing, they envy – either consciously or unconsciously – everyone who is born in the West. They envy the well-ordered life there and the fact that for people in the West, everything is more or less plannable, predictable, controllable, and possible. It is not so much a question of the economic aspects as it is of the respect as a person. At the same time, both Russians and Ukrainians suffer, up to the present day, from their past, during which they were programmed, from which they couldn't escape, and which was characterized by "carrot and stick".

Money and material prosperity offer only limited security. Just as rapidly as they come, they can disappear again, is their philosophy. But the stick remains, like a yoke, under which they must suffer and from which no escape is possible. In many cases, the suffering is more mental than physical. Even someone with money and influence cannot escape from the conditions into which he was born. Someone who has achieved power practices the rule of a pecking order and applies pressure to the next lower level. Modest prosperity is begrudged even the best neighbor, as an often told story from Siberia proves: A family owns a cow which gives milk. The neighbor has no cow. Instead of asking for some milk and perhaps offering to help care for and feed the cow, he kills it. Now no one has milk. The period when the czars ruled and the seventy years of the Soviet regime have left permanent traces. The ordinary people were always humbled and subjugated by the ruling class and the authorities. That seems to be embedded in their genes. The people suffer under their own social system. They also suffer under their new rulers, under force, pressure, and corruption, and cannot free themselves. Up to the present day, they can only partially fulfill their potential. Everyday life consumes them and robs them of their energy. Daily, one or the other stumbling block must be gotten out of the way and problems must be solved as well as possible to bring a little "order" into one's own life. They are practiced in juggling the unpredictable. The ability to improvise is enormous. That is why they are, as a rule, more ingenious than people from the West.

One thing is certain: The unforeseeable always occurs, in all areas and from all sides. Of course, in Ukraine, this world view also influences politics and business. Western partners suffer under the fact that agreements which have been met often begin to falter. Generally I discriminate between two types of people – first, "people as such" and second, people in or with a function. The people as such are usually good, hospitable, and helpful. The people with functions in the administration and agencies are often calculating and driven by self-interest. An individual person can readily be encountered in both roles. That does not make the situation any easier. I do not know if true understanding is possible. All too often, my understanding was taken advantage of. When I tried to accommodate them, I was outwitted For example, craftsmen who were renovating my apartment in Kiev, with the support of much vodka, had to be removed with the help of the police. After a while, so-called partners stab you in the back – and that didn't only happen to me alone. The best people can turn into the worst enemies, especially when they feel that their national pride has been injured. Not everyone can accept criticism.

A guest is given everything. But the guest can only go this far and no further. He is not seen as an equal, but is, rather, treated as a kind of king, a privileged person who, for a certain length of time, is admitted to the circle of locals. He is not, however, allowed to delve deeper into their lives.

Am I running in circles? Again? Isn't it possible to find a general answer to my questions? Are fragments of feelings all that remain, laid together in the course of more than twenty years in a mosaic, with constantly changing colors and patterns, like a kaleidoscope, giving me the runaround? In the beginning, I cried after every trip to Ukraine and didn't understand why. Today it is clear. It was the culture shock, tied to the feeling of helplessness. I would have liked so much to help all the people that I met, to find their own way. And I have to accept the fact that I can't alter anyone's fate, but can only, at best, write about it and publish it. But then ... has my mood hit rock bottom? Let them all go to the devil. The fat faces with the shifty eyes; the functionaries with their big bellies, which can barely be covered by their coats and threaten to pop the buttons. I have no compassion with those people who say one thing and do another, who are always complaining and secretly hoarding supplies, who can no longer distinguish between honest and dishonest. No, I can no longer encourage anyone to come here, and I don't want to either. Each person must have his own experiences. You just have to have money. With money, everything happens, everything becomes possible. This run-down country no longer interests me. I am tired of writing about the eternally malfunctioning politics or businesses, about the intrigues and the unethical profiteers. I want to build something up and not just have obstacles constantly placed in my path.

It's the first time since I have been traveling to the former Soviet Union that I feel like this. It's the year 1997 and I am heading toward my fortieth birthday. The people don't mean anything to me any more. But still ... there are a few who are important to me. Zurab, for example, from Georgia. And the others. But I can't stand the smells any more, or the pushing and shoving in the metro. The romance is over. But why? What was the reason? I just don't want to any more. Not even for money. I only want to go home, to a clean white bed and a proper job; I don't want to try to explain paradoxes any more. I can no longer stand the sight of them – the old bowed women with their heavy wool socks. I don't want to have to smell them anymore – the peculiar mixtures of mothballs, sour food, and Soviet perfume. I want to go home. I hate the crumbled particle boards at the hairdresser's; the filthy sink that looks as though it hasn't been cleaned for three weeks. I hate all of it. But I am also touched when I see how happy Marina, the hairdresser, is over the two dollars (in 2000) that I give her for washing and cutting my hair.

I can't change anything. No one can change anything. The country must be left to itself. My dream has reached its end, live, and right in the middle. I no longer hope and I no longer wish. I observe and leave things be. Good luck, Seryozha.

But old love doesn't die. Was it all just an illusion? My feelings not real? What happened to the morale which was just at a low point? I hardly know myself, as my glance lingers with a warm heart on the bleached-out wood of the window shutters. Longingly I look through the lighted windows, see the traditional carpets on the walls, the old aluminum flatware, and people who are obviously not cold because they have moved closer together. People who do not yet have the ideal of individualism. Suddenly the mixture of bad gasoline, poor-quality tobacco, and mothballs smells good again and I am pleased by the otherness, by the foreignness, which is also so familiar.

Am I a victim of my feelings? Are all my senses still working properly? Where is the paradox? Can a person from the West only endure Ukraine to a certain extent? Yes. A simple 'yes' is enough. A person who stays there too long is overcome by the conditions. And this even with the best of intentions. Much is certainly a question of money. Someone who can draw from an expense account is definitely better off than someone who has come of their own accord and lives at the grassroots level.

Anyone who plans a business, the opening of an office or any kind of cooperation with a Ukrainian company, should plan to spend at least fifty percent more time than would normally be needed in Germany. And a little sense of adventure is required, as demonstrated by the case of the young German orchestra conductor who met a Ukrainian woman in Odessa and lived together with her for at least two years, from a monthly local salary, roughly equal to six dollars. In those days, in the early Nineties, that was still possible, a thing that no one today can imagine. And he just barely managed with that amount. First he was in Kiev, at the conservatory, as an intern, to experience things there which weren't possible in the West. Above all, he wanted to gain experience in conducting. It was later, in Odessa, where he was on his own, that he experienced the ruptured social structure at first hand. At the time, I interviewed him and asked him what he wished for. I chose "Wie geschmiert, so geklungen" ("A well-greased sound") as the title for an article about this man. During his venture to make honest music in Odessa, the young conductor's illusions were destroyed, piece by piece. He learned how corruptible honor, professional ethics, standards, and performance quality can frequently be there and how corruption can influence the music and its performance.

A WELL-GREASED SOUND*

The press is bribed, the orchestra bought. Music becomes a product, the quality of which depends on the amount of the prices paid. Contemporary music is even stifled entirely by the old corrupt structures, which leave no room for reforms or experiments.

Naive and full of illusions, the conducting adventurer from Germany traveled to Ukraine. Two years later he has become hardened but he has remained. His biography can be quickly told: instruction in trumpet, piano, organ, and cello; conservatory in Stuttgart; courses with Sergiu Celibidache; the conducting of various concerts; formation of a chamber orchestra; state examinations in the subjects piano, vocal music, and conducting; concert tours; voice coach and choir director of a choir in Southern Germany – all in all a solid education without much practical experience. That's why he

---

* Published/broadcast in the early Nineties by several German newspapers and radio stations.

accepted an offer that resulted from private contacts – a kind of internship at the conservatory in Kiev. That was an intermediate stop on the way to the opera in Odessa, where he has been living for two years. Resolutely he became involved in a collapsed social structure, in which standards no longer exist and where money makes everything possible. Youthful obstinacy and maybe a principled attitude quickly collided with corruption. During the entire two years he received no mention in the press, "because I didn't pay. I find it disgusting that I have to give someone money to make him react to the fact that I am even here." Aside from all moral considerations, in any case his average monthly income, to the value of six dollars, isn't enough to pay any bribes. From the approximately 20,000 Ukrainian karbovanets (that was the name of the transition currency in those days, following the Russian rubel and preceding today's hryvnya) that he earns, depending on the level of inflation, he can afford at best a meal for two in one of the new private restaurants. Even when the conductor adds roughly twenty dollars from his own pocket every month, it's still not much. Clothing or high-quality food products can only be bought with foreign currency or insanely high amounts of karbovanets. A kilo of good meat costs approximately 6,000 karbovanets. That is roughly a third of his monthly income. After two years, the German no longer thinks about the fact that he only saves the equivalent of twenty or thirty German pfennig. But he notices very rapidly that it costs 40 times more in nerves.

The young conductor got acquainted with life in Ukraine, from the bottom up. For a time, he dwelt more than lived in the filth of a student residence. Later he lived together with his girlfriend, sharing eight square meters (approx. 86 square feet) until they could move into the two-room apartment in Odessa. The elation is at an end when he sees daily how human values lose importance in a society which has not yet replaced the old commando system with democratic rules of the game; in which the mafia reigns, and the majority of the new businesspeople shortsightedly line their own pockets. The fact that he pays no bribes makes him almost suspicious. Some people laugh at him, others marvel, while still others, "fear me because they think that if I can manage without it then I must have an incredibly large hand at my back." The fact that he tells his story so openly seems almost dangerous to him. He prudently left his address off his business card. He doesn't own a telephone.

The musical experiences are also ambiguous. Corruption and the decline of values have also infected the sound, like a malignant tumor. The musicians play according to how much they are paid. For 20,000 karbovanets, which is also their approximate monthly wage, they allow themselves to be quieted by a poor conductor who wouldn't have a chance in his own country. On the other hand, they have no fear of the young German, who is considered an intern, who doesn't use the power of money, and is not supported by the directors of the opera. "They tell me unabashedly: If you always beat (conduct) like that, we don't understand it. That is painful, but instructive."

Yes, I somehow feel the same way. Every day in Ukraine means a new pain, a new lesson. Once again, a stay is approaching its end. Once again it is time to depart. Each time I am accompanied by doubts. I have the feeling that I am leaving a heap of ruins behind. And I consider turning my back on the country forever to finally work again at home in Germany. I weep. Large tears roll down my cheeks. A heap of ruins? Have I been unable to build anything? Not even my own little correspondent's office? Of course I did. I set up the infrastructure that I needed. I have many contacts. That's not the problem. It is simply the frustration of knowing that here nothing functions like I need it to in order to earn a normal profit with my stories. And I think about those who preceded me and maybe also those who will follow – business people who have abandoned their intentions because the mafia, the state, or maybe just the momentary circumstances, the conditions, interfered. I am sitting and looking at the colorful curtains next to my desk area in the little apartment on Klovskiy Spusk in Kiev. I look at the trees across the street and I know already that I will miss the many chestnut trees that bloom so wonderfully in the Ukrainian capital every year, and also the giant fields of sunflowers…
How often have I crossed the Dnepr (Ukrainian:

Dnipro), over the metro bridge, or driven to the left bank over the Paton Bridge (*Most Patona*). How often did I go for a fitting to my dear seamstress, Tamara, who used to only sew for the upper elite of the Soviet Union. She was a wonderful woman, always brash. She always spoke up and criticized the politicians. The women in Ukraine, yes, they always impressed me. And I wondered how the usually beautiful women could have such unprepossessing husbands. But there were no others. In those days, at the end of the Nineties, I became acquainted with Kira Shakhova, professor for world literature at Kiev's Shevchenko University, visited her, and wrote an article about women. It appeared in 1999 in the *Trierischer Volksfreund* newspaper, two pages even, and in the magazine "*Weibblick*".

WOMEN LIKE SMALL ARMORED VEHICLES

... Yes, Ms. Shakhova knew how Ukraine could be helped to get more respect abroad. And if there could be more active, energetic, and, above all, educated women and men like her, Ukraine would surely appear in a very different light. But since education is expensive and doesn't offer a quick profit, like short-term business deals do, the intellectual elite are pushed aside. Due to the economic difficulties of Ukraine, only a few, like Kira Shakhova, are in a position to continue with academic teaching and research. In the center of Kiev, she lives in one of the beautiful old, ornamented houses, on the fourth floor. She opens the door, wearing tights. She hadn't expected the visitor this early. Calmly she pulls

on the black jeans. She smooths the thin, red-and-black patterned pullover, over which she is wearing a black leather vest and a necklace of large red beads, with a matching heavy, red, oval ring and matching earrings. Her long gray hair is elegantly pinned together at the neck. She invites me into her living room, the middle room of three. Kira Shakhova is cosmopolitan and well-read. The rooms are crowded with books. Pictures she painted hang on the walls, leaving barely a piece of wallpaper visible. Painting is her hobby, when she has the time and inspiration to do so, during the vacation in the summer months. She never sells any of her watercolors, sketches, icons, and miniatures, she immediately wards off any inquiry. In the kitchen, she sets the old teakettle on the stove and serves tea in battered mugs. The refrigerator is worn, one chair is broken, the wallpaper is torn and yellowed and underneath it the plaster is crumbling. The sink bears the marks of decades of use. But Kira Shakhova is above such everyday concerns. Tidying up is simply necessary occasionally, but not important to her. For her, life obviously plays in a different realm. Her thoughts never seem to stand still. Her animated eyes captivate you, while she talks about the motherhood cult in Ukraine, for me an entirely new topic. "In Ukraine, the cult of the mothers is somehow especially sacred." What is the origin? The psychologists and ethnologists sometimes have fairly strange explanations and even derive from them the idea that this cult of women and mothers somehow makes the Ukrainian people weak and docile.

Yes, all Ukrainians, both men and women, are forbearing. But can this be attributed to the motherhood cult, when it is the woman who always bears the whole load? Ms Shakhova is skeptical. But one thing is clear: Modern times are brutally different and demand a complete adjustment of all people and their values. Formerly, Ukraine was Russified by the Soviet power and the perspective was therefore clear. Since the collapse of the Soviet Union and the independence of Ukraine in 1991, an orientation to characteristic, Ukrainian values is lacking. Old standards no longer apply and new ones have not yet been found. Kira Shakhova is an unusual modern woman who is successfully coming to terms with the new circumstances. But unfortunately there are still, "very many limitations from the former life." All of a sudden one can see, "the old ears sticking up.

Sunflowers extend to the horizon

But I am an optimist. I always say that we have to wait a little. Only rabbits and kittens are born rapidly. And we have been a free state for such a short time."

What would be different in Ukraine if women were in charge? Would the Chernobyl catastrophe have happened? Would there be the miners' strikes in the Donbas region of East Ukraine, corruption, economic crisis, and the nationalistic confrontations between East, West, and South Ukraine if women had responsibility for the political and economic restructuring of Ukraine? What if? And what chances do Ukrainian women have today, to intervene in the policies of their country? According to the revolutionary vision of the clairvoyant, Lilya Efimovna, published in the Ukrainian newspaper, Boulevard, one of three women with a special karma will be President of Ukraine in the period

Dnipro, up to five kilometers wide

of office that follows this one. This woman is intelligent, decent, and sufficiently known in political circles, explains Lyudmila. *Beginning in 1998, Ukraine will experience an economic upswing and unprecedented stability. Everything will take a turn for the better. Under this President, "in approximately ten or fifteen years, Ukraine will have that life which we have so long been wishing for."*

The prophecy got mixed reactions, but most women agreed on one thing – that everything would be better if they were in power. They thought that women were more flexible and open-minded in respect to global politics and global economy. Women had unimagined abilities. For example, Kira Shakhova, professor for world literature, had observed that women in politics and business were usually energetic and relatively stout, not especially young, and that they mostly looked like "small armored vehicles. These ladies can do everything." A Russian poet once described what also applies to women in Ukrainian villages; they could "stop a running horse and enter a burning house." And that was exactly how these businesswomen were. "They can do everything." A representative of a foreign foundation commented about the women with which she works, "I love them. They are wonderful!"

Yes, I want to return, to Kiev, to carry on. The topics that I researched have been marketed. When I am in Germany I long to go to Kiev again. It is a constant emotional roller coaster. That is the only explanation that I have for the warmth that I feel when, upon my return, I look at the shutters with the flaked paint or inhale the hated (when I have been there too long) smell of bad gasoline.... Am I crazy? I yearn to leave then return so gladly? Like all the foreign nationals? When I have just arrived I view everything with detachment and a warm heart. When I have stayed longer than the appropriate time (and that varies), the conditions overcome me and I can no longer deal with them. Mind you, I always mean the conditions at the grassroots. It is all a question of money. Those who have enough can also afford more amenities.

During the course of time, I have met many other Germans in Kiev. More and more German companies have established joint ventures in Ukraine, opened a branch office, or whatever they thought appropriate. The occasional swashbuckler was also involved. A few of the Germans who got in at the beginning allowed themselves unusual "jokes". When they were too fed up with daily life or when they didn't like the way things were going, they ingeniously "got revenge". I described the activity of two such men as a contribution for a German radio broadcaster in the early Nineties.

"If you shake it in the box, it gets dizzy and can no longer run so fast. Meanwhile, I'll make a big to-do and you will rant about the sanitary facilities, etc." No sooner said than done. This situation is taking place in one of

Kiev's more posh restaurants in Kiev, the Napoleon, in the Nineties. The problem is, as is so often the case, that the price-performance ratio is poor. The quality of the food is at best equal to that of a one-star restaurant but the prices are as high as those with three stars. This upsets Yupp and Dieter every time. And it's not only that. Actually, it's life in Ukraine in general that bothers them. Admittedly, they accept the conditions, but they can't – and don't want to – resign themselves to the fact that a person can be stopped on the street, randomly and arbitrarily, because of uncommitted offenses, ostensible offenses against the traffic regulations. Or that the Ukrainian employees in their company don't toe the line or work in an organized way; that chaos rules the country and laws are interpreted at personal discretion. But they play along and develop strategies for dealing with life in Ukraine. They loudly comment on everything that doesn't happen like they think it should. And just like two small boys at an adventure playground, they think up all kinds of pranks, to get even with the Ukrainians. There – suddenly the dizzied cockroach jumps out of the matchbox. "Hey, waiter, where is your boss?" one of the two men calls. The waiter is confused, assures them that there are no cockroaches in this restaurant and doesn't know what to say. The small insect has recovered and scurries quickly away. The two men are laughing up their sleeves.

I really had some experiences with these guys. Once I drove together with one of them from Kiev to Lugansk

(Ukrainian: Luhansk). A large, formerly Soviet, truck transport company was having an anniversary. It's a long drive. It's winter. The road is icy and before long it happens. A dumb accident. The other driver is at fault. He skidded into us because he didn't have winter tires. It takes forever for the police to come. Then endless discussions. Reports must be made. There we stand and cannot continue on our way. It's clear, the other man apparently offers money, to get out of the situation. The German doesn't want to offer money. Terrible! Late in the evening we arrive in Lugansk and fall into bed, in order to be fit for the reception the next morning. And it begins right away, early the next day, with *butterbrody* (Russian for sandwiches), bacon, vodka – a sumptuous buffet. No, this time I don't want vodka, and take sparkling wine, Shampanskoye. But oh dear, I bitterly regret it. Before very long I am as sick as a dog. I dash to the toilet and spew up as much as I can. I won't forget the rule that I learned there: Only with the help of vodka can this food be tolerated. In Ukrainian it's called "Horilka" and is feminine, because it ends in an a. Again and again I am confronted with vodka. The enjoyment of a pleasant glass of wine hardly ever happens in Ukraine. In the first place, it's too expensive, and secondly, in these years the Ukrainians can't really be called wine connoisseurs and buy only sweet wine, which might be drunk with dessert. So I prefer to drink vodka. If it's not accompanied by any other alcohol, and when it's washed down with fruit juice or compote, it can be tolerated well. It's really true that vodka is like a kind of ink, with which a contract is sealed. Frequently, business partners serve some after a meeting.

And then there are the toasts. There is a set procedure with vodka. And you can learn quite a bit about the people in the process. I also take part and adapt to always telling something in detail before emptying the glass. The first toast is always drunk by the host to the guests. Next it's the turn of the most "prominent" of the invited guests. The third toast is always drunk to the women, beginning with the "lady of the house". Everyone has a turn. But it can be exhausting when the procedure gets out of control, because of too many guests and too great a quantity of vodka.

Interview in the country

So it is that I muddle my way through the correspondent years, always on the lookout and on the trail of interesting stories, searching for life and for that special topic which can be sold well in Germany, as an article or radio feature. Among others, the transport possibilities – airlines, trains, and automobile – were such topics.

A party in my first apartment in Kiev in 1997

The musician Rudik shows the amount of vodka to be in a glas

The car from "HiPP"

To Kiev by car

It was the first time. HiPP, the baby food manufacturer, had given me an Audi 100, to transfer to Kiev. Nikolaus Hipp is himself a fan of Eastern Europe and in return for driving the car to Kiev, I got to use it for three months. I didn't realize what I had gotten myself into. The papers alone – that in itself was a challenge back then, more than twenty years ago. There were two of us. A former HiPP employee from the Transcarpathian region was also driving his own Audi 100 to Uzhhorod. Zoltan always drove quite fast. In a two-car convoy we sped along the autobahn from Munich to Vienna, then on through Hungary (in those days the autobahn didn't extend as far as it does today), to the Ukrainian border. I no longer remember exactly how we crossed the border. In any case there were difficulties.

Actually, I wasn't allowed to import a car which didn't belong to me. To do that, I would have had to have different papers. After long discussions – and I think that my co-driver might have helped a little then – we could finally cross the border after all. Right away, on the first day in Ukraine, in Uzhgorod (Ukrainian: Uzhhorod) the customs plates were removed from the car. By the militia, of course. Because something was not quite right about the way the car was being imported. I was scared stiff. It was the first time that I had experienced such a thing. Thank heavens that I was not yet alone.

Zoltan helped me get the license plates back from the militia. I think that we paid them something.

The ten year-old-car ran well. In Kiev I had parked it outside the window of my apartment, in a kind of rear courtyard, attached an immobilizer to the steering wheel and clutch, and looked repeatedly out the window, to check that everything was okay. At night I was especially uneasy. At the least little noise I jumped out of bed and peered into the dark, to see if someone was maybe tampering with the car. No – and I lay down again. Sometimes that happened a couple of times in one night. At some point I got a little calmer but the worry never stopped entirely.

Back then there was always a bottle of vodka next to the hand brake and in the glove compartment there were always a few ballpoint pens and cigarette lighters. At the time, those were the instruments with which the militia in Ukraine could be placated if you had been driving too fast or had otherwise committed a real or alleged traffic violation. Several years later this no longer helped. Then the police wanted to see money. For quite a while, approximately twenty Ukrainian Hryvnya (between 1.5 and 2 euros, depending on the exchange rate) was the standard rate for speeding violations. At some point, this sum increased by a power of ten. Meanwhile, I am no longer acquainted with the rate because the prices continually rise and the exchanges rates change. Public authorities always have more leverage. And people are happy when they can just continue on their way. The Ukrainians have a kind of black humor. If this situation can't be changed, then, despite the serious nature, jokes are told about it, like this one:

VACATION AT THE EXPENSE OF THE MILITIA*

The policeman is standing by the edge of the street, just as he does every day. He lets his thoughts wander and reflects how high the fine could be that he will demand from the next driver who commits a violation. Before long, a heavy limousine with tinted windows approaches, clearly breaking the speed limit. The traffic officer waves the car to the side, with his stick. The procedure is rapid. The driver stops, lowers one of the darkly tinted window panes slightly, and slips a ten dollar bill through the tiny slit. The driver can't be seen. The policeman takes the bill and gives the driver a sign that he can continue driving. The next day, everything is repeated. The limousine drives along the same route, at excessive speed. The policeman waves the driver to the side. The car stops. The driver again lowers the window a crack and pushes a ten dollar bill out. The policeman signals the driver on his way. This is also repeated on the following day and on the fourth and fifth days, for a whole week, two weeks, three and four weeks, one month, two months, a third month....

Suddenly, the car fails to appear. The policeman scans the street for a whole day. On the second day, still no

---

* A joke about the police

sign of the limousine. The same is true for the third and fourth days. This turns into a whole week, then two, and finally a whole month has passed. One day, there he is again – the speeder. At the same spot, the vehicle approaches the policeman at high speed. He waves his stick. The driver pulls off to the right, lowers the tinted window a crack, and pushes a ten-dollar bill through the window. The policeman demands,
"Open the window a little wider! Where were you?"
"I was on vacation, on the Canary Islands," answers the driver
"So, so," says the policeman. "You were on vacation on the Canaries at my expense and with my money."

Was I driving too fast?

This joke makes the rounds. And somehow it contains a kernel of truth. I can understand that people in Ukraine, especially civil servants but also professors and others who don't earn much, stipulate their own "fees" as a kind of salary increase. Of course, that is only a small form of corruption, where millions or even billions flow in its large form. But what should they do? The fish begins stinking at its head ….

I'm curious whether or not the Ukrainians will ever come to terms with corruption. This mechanism is too deeply rooted. And those who have once had a place at the trough don't want to leave again, no matter which branch or agency they belong to.

I also get some money from a different source. And that is unusual for me. I get it from "my" musicians.

My band and I

We play in the park

The saxophone part

My Band and I

I feel like a clochard. Under the bridge is the best place. The people are tilted at an angle determined by the amount of vodka. All taken together, it must be a couple of liters that we drank – the musicians and I. Now we're standing under the bridge. I let my thoughts wander, thinking about how a film could be shot here: a rainy day, the Western advertising signs shine across the street. It's six in the evening, twilight. We have been standing here and drinking since midday. In the vodka-induced intoxication, the first argument begins. They don't always drink so much. But today.... The musicians get together once a week and when I'm in Kiev I join them. I always take my saxophone mouthpiece along and the instrument, a tenor sax is loaned to me by Rudik during my stays in Kiev. At first we played in Mariinskyj Park, close to the center of town, not far from the Parliament and near the beautiful palace of the same name. Later, we also played in Nivki Park, in the western part of Kiev. First a two-hour outdoor concert for strollers, then a friendly get-together on a park bench or, if it rains, under the bridge. They are all professional musicians who play in Kiev's various orchestras and who get together in their leisure time in order to do something besides playing only in the opera orchestra, symphony orchestra, jazz combo or chamber music ensemble. On weekends they get out their oldest instrument and play for the passersby. I am happy and proud that I can read music well enough to play along right away. And I am immensely happy that I am allowed to join in. For me, it is one of the few possibilities to unwind in Kiev with its three million inhabitants. We found one another right at the beginning of my time in Kiev. I wanted to also follow my hobbies in Ukraine and live at least a little as I did in Germany – in other words, play music, do sports, and the other things that I do to relax in Germany. A musician in my group of friends helped me get in touch with the band.

After playing the music, we head to the park bench. They unpack sausage, salt pickles or sour pickles, tomatoes, and of course Ukrainian bacon and vodka. Everything is very informal and I am entirely included. With music and among musicians that's easy, straightforward, and perfectly natural. I am also included when the drummer, Yura, says, "Music simply unites us – cheers!" Earlier everyone could afford to go to a restaurant after making music. But now (the early Nineties) that's no longer possible.

Of all the professions, a musician earns the least. I write a report about music education and the Kiev conservatory. I want to know how things are there. After all, music is my favorite topic. At this point in time, 1,200 students are registered. "Music is the only thing that keeps you going," is the opinion of a young woman who wants to be a violinist. I am astonished and a little confused by the fatalistic commitment of these students to music and art. "I cannot see any way out of the situation," says one. "I can't learn a new profession. I have been involved with music for six years, just for myself. But if we don't do it, the art will continue to decline." The chances of earning an acceptable income with their profession are exceedingly poor for the students of the Kiev conservatory. The standard of living lies at the lowest limit. That is why not only students but also professors, and teachers in general, are forced to find other sources of income. For example, they sell clothing at the market to keep their heads economically above water. In Ukraine, music can't support anyone. Why then, time and again, young people summon up the needed energy to begin, and also end, musical training at one of the twenty-five conservatories, can simply be explained by music itself, explains one female student: "It is the only thing that helps you live. When you are playing, you forget everything." Some students receive a scholarship. At this time, in the early Nineties, this amounted to between 300,000 and a little less than 500,00 kupons* per month. The converted values are approximately between four and six German marks. The most talented of the 1,200 students, at the time fourteen male and female students, received 790,000 Kupons – not quite ten German marks a month – with which the Ukrainian Ministry for Culture wanted to promote their abilities. In comparison: During the same time, a 2-pound bread cost the equivalent of 20

---

* Kupon or karbovanets is the name of the transition currency used in Ukraine in the years between 1992 and 1996.

pfennig and a pair of shoes cost maybe twenty to thirty German marks. Without the support of newly rich Ukrainian patrons or foreign sponsors and endowments, much wouldn't even have been possible. And the same is still true today.

But despite all economic difficulties, today young musicians and singers of both sexes from Ukraine repeatedly receive first prizes in international competitions. For a long time they weren't recognized because anyone who came from the countries in the area of the former Soviet Union was usually called a Russian. And earlier, people could only travel to the West for competitions and concerts through the bottleneck of Moscow, or, in other words, with express permission of *Gosconcert* the existing governmental Soviet concert agency. The conservatories themselves were seen as branches of Moscow, somewhere out in the "provinces", even though the Kiev conservatory, established in 1913, has produced as many top-ranking musicians as Moscow has. It was founded by the Russian music society before the October Revolution and the ensuing Soviet Union and was just called the music college. After several restructurings, it was renamed the Peter Tchaikovsky Conservatory in 1940. The pianist, Vladimir Horowitz, studied here. Hermann Neuhaus, a famous piano educator, founded his school in Kiev. Many of those who were called Russian stars had their start in Kiev. But, Moscow, as the hub of the former Soviet Union, offered young musicians, after their education, better opportunities to conquer the international stage. Fortunately, that has all changed. In the course of my reports, I have always made an effort to tell the German public more about Ukrainian musicians. I am proud of them all. Some I know personally, such as the conductor, Oksana Lyniv, from Lviv (Lemberg) and Odessa, who conducts the orchestra of the Bavarian National Opera, in Munich. Or the bass, singer, Aleksander Tsymbalyuk, from Odessa, who sings in Hamburg; the conductor, Roman Kofman, left Kiev to conduct the orchestra of the Beethovenhalle in Bonn; the top-ranking soprano, Victoria Loukjanetz, primadonna at the Vienna National Opera; and many more – including those in the rock and pop music scene. The singer, dancer, producer, composer, and activist, Ruslana Lyzhychko, won the Eurovision Song Contest and The received the

The conservatory in Kiev

World Music Award in 2004. The list is much too long to do them all credit here.

Oh yes, I don't want to forget Anatol and Sasha (a different Sasha). I have to mention them, also friends of mine. Anatol plays domra, a kind of balalaika, and Sasha plays button accordion – two highly qualified super musicians! They often traveled through Germany, making music, in the summer. They didn't mind standing on the street, playing music, and waiting for donations. I helped them give a performance here and there and sometimes also negotiated a payment. And when I was feeling good, I joined them and sang along. That was a wonderful time. From the money which they earned this way during the three months of summer, they could live for the rest of the year, and

Here privately ...

even save a little. Of course, the high cost to them was that they were forced to live without their families. I always like to look back on the many wonderful hours that I shared with them. Music is a kind of elixir of life. I also come alive when I hear the sound of "my band" in Kiev. There is no end to the joy I experience, making music with these men – primarily because of the music itself, but that's not all. There is more to it. The human vibrations make common understanding possible. We are friends. How often has Gosha, the leader of the band, offered me help when he noticed that I wasn't doing well, when I had problems with my job or with life in Ukraine in general? But how could he have helped me? I always felt the limits very clearly. Emotional warmth – yes, but practical help was just not possible, because of the situation. And so

... and here publicly

we make music together, including on this, the fiftieth anniversary of the victory over the German fascists. Close by, a Ukrainian official is giving a lofty speech about the brave soldiers who conquered the Germans, back then in the Second World War. Meanwhile, I am sitting together with Ukrainian musicians, playing together with them in the same key. I will later drink the same vodka together with them and after the performance, will get the same small payment as each of them – to a value of maybe five German marks. We look at one another and grin to ourselves. No, politics or division never played a role for us. I clearly recognized that humanity means friendship and still more, international friendship.

The column, topped by Ukrainka, in Kiev's center

Media conference in Yalta, when Crimea was still Ukrainian

Freedom of the press

This topic became important shortly after Ukrainian independence. Everyone was euphoric about bringing freedom of the press to a young, independent Ukraine. Of course I, at the time not quite forty years old, was also involved – right at the forefront. After all, I also wanted to firmly anchor the democracy and bring Western guiding principles to Ukraine.

Back then I was still convinced that there really was such a thing as a free press, at least in Germany. I jumped on the bandwagon, which promised – and brought – seminars, good professional fees, and not least of all a job as consultant for media policy in Kiev.

Ukrainian journalists were to learn the craft of journalism, work professionally, and not just pour verbal "dirt" over the politicians. Together with the newspapers *Den, Argumenty i Fakty, Zerkalo Nedeli, Fakty; Svoboda, Ukraina Moloda*, and many more we, the Center of the Free Press in Kiev, as the Ukrainian partner, and I, cooperated.

Together with the German Embassy in Kiev, with other embassies, and with the Delegation of the European Union, we offered seminars. I played various roles, as organizer, moderator or lecturer. It was an exciting time. The journalists learned the right way to ask questions and the press spokespeople, positions which were just then being established, learned how to answer questions. The meaning of sharing information with media representatives, and that this is a part of a democracy, was something that was not yet known. In the former Soviet Union, information was more often obscured than openly disclosed. The journalists were all grateful and I was happy that I could be useful here. The logical follow-up to these activities was that I became a consultant for media policy and for three years I built up and led the project to establish the Academy of Ukrainian Press (AUP). But it was also hard-earned money. There was practically no budget. More than once I had to accept hearing the AUP compared to large political foundations and to listen to criticism of myself, as director. Actually, I had at least five different jobs in this small business, as I would call the AUP: director, accountant, PR woman, trainer for colleagues, lecturer, seminar leader, and more. I even painted our first office white and installed lamps – and ended up with bloody fingers in the process. But it was also a wonderful time filled with activity, thanks to the many jobs and functions. Then, at some point, it was no longer possible. It was just too much. The shining eyes of my Ukrainian colleagues, happy about the seminars and materials which they received from us, could no longer make up for my exhaustion in this job. The Ukrainian counterpart felt squelched by me. There were personal and professional problems. I was simply run down. Finally, I just became ill, physically and emotionally. And the emotional aspect hurt the most. I just wanted to teach values, like those that applied in Germany, teach a professional craft, and just be in Ukraine, with "my" people, motivated by love. I used the compulsory break after the end of the contract and project, which had often been extended for only three months at a time but which had lasted a total of three years, to spin a new grid, this time to Odessa.

The opera house and I and my first book

Odessa

Generally speaking, I never understood jokes well. I felt like people were pulling my leg, I was angry, slow on the uptake, or didn't understand anything at all. And then I came to Odessa, of all places, to this crazy city. There, where you are always the object of a joke. How hard I worked here, to apply my knowledge and my experience from Germany, as musicologist and woman of the press! I was to be responsible for public relations, and even more for international contacts, at the wonderful opera. Back then, in 2004, the theater had not yet been renovated but the building still cast a spell over me. And even today I still think of the legendary bass singer, Shalyapin, and of Pushkin's words, "I would stay in Odessa, if only because of the opera." It was the same with me. How happy I was, how proud of this theater, and how I strove to get this fantastic job!

And then the problems which gradually began brewing and the looming disappointment. Things won't happen the way I want them to. Odessa is corrupt. The directors of the opera change rapidly. One a year. How can artistic development take place then? I still try however, once again against my better knowledge and judgment. It must be possible. If I come with all my expertise, with my knowledge, my drive, I the motor .... Then something must be possible to accomplish.

But life proves me wrong. Try as I can, the contract with the opera doesn't come about. Suddenly, no one feels responsible. When it starts becoming concrete, nobody dares to do anything. Not until much later do I discover that someone else is behind all these denial strategies, namely the then governor of Odessa. That is so long ago that I don't need to mention the name here. But he had his own plans for the opera. He wanted to become the director and boycotted all innovations. And behind this was once again the desire – representative for many similar cases – to make money from the situation. Somehow the institutions always leave loopholes for corrupt dealings.

Ignorant of this, I believe all alleged remarks, am even sympathetic, show understanding, and I found a society, the Society of the Friends of the Odessa Opera. I become the director and begin my work. Once again I tighten my ties to Ukraine; once again there are many difficulties – although the wonderful opera house would almost sell itself, if those responsible would only have a real interest in it. Sometimes I really feel as if things are unreal. Like in the opera house itself, where the scenery on the inside is somehow grotesque. I watch the rehearsal for *The Secret Marriage* by Cimarosa. The director is unknown, a radio is playing in the third section, carpenters are tapping and hammering. And during all this, on the stage, Carolina kisses her secret lover, Paolino. That's everyday life here. Artists rehearse in a magnificent opera house under conditions which would have long caused musicians and singers in Germany to protest and stop performances. Why? The opera house was under renovation for twelve years. This wonderful theater, designed by the Viennese architects, Fellner and Helmer, and erected in the years between 1884 and 1887, threatened to sink. The construction materials for the city, built more than two hundred years ago, were taken from under the ground upon which the buildings were placed. The resulting widely branching network of subterranean catacombs attracts tourists today. In any case, it is supposed to be the cavities, the uneven stresses of the three-story building, and also the slipping of the loess which are responsible for the approximately fifty-thousand-ton weight pushing continuously to the sea. The demise of the theater has been predicted more than once. But that is clearly an exaggeration explains one of the former opera directors and calculates that, according to statistics, the entire city is sliding toward the sea at the rate of two millimeters a year. That creates hairline cracks in walls, which, incidentally, appear again and again in all of Odessa. One of the directors also explains, "We can hold on here for several more thousands of years. There's no reason to panic." The more the building is threatened, the more the musicians and singers campaign for its preservation, notwithstanding the fact that they are powerless against corrupt machinations. Everywhere where building or renovating is taking place, monies are also being channeled off. Then the windows just have to be installed two or three times, the floor renovated several times, etc. It took a long time for me to comprehend that. But since 2007 that beautiful theater is finally finished.

It is in conjunction with, and in, this opera house and also in the Philharmonia that I become acquainted with the high-society of Odessa. There they come, the women with their orange-colored hair, ornately polished nails, in long or extremely short skirts, and in any case always looking very creative. Of course, I also experience their business practices when I'm soliciting members for the society *Friends of the Opera* or hoping for other cultural support. Maybe I just met the wrong people but somehow it always seemed to me that they

On the great gala stairway

were afraid to really stand up for something; that they were somehow shrinking back. Or is it because I am German? But Odessa, of all places, is a multicultural city in which one-hundred-and-thirty or more ethnic minorities live and which offers an opportunity to everyone. Why not also to me? Yes, I have to be involved. I want to be involved. I have something to say and something to give; something that must be heard. So keep running, motor. The opera is worth it; the people are worth it. Meanwhile, I have made friends in Odessa. They encourage me; they admire me and my drive. We open an office next to the opera. It is my own office, that I put at our disposal, and sell again later. But that doesn't have to be announced to the whole world. It is a real battle. Who is stronger? The *Friends of the Opera*, under my direction, that absolutely want to do something worthwhile, or the management of the opera? The answer is clear. In the big machine, I am only a tiny wheel. But maybe I am one whose rotating produces an effect? A former colleague even suggested once that the people of Odessa should name a street or a lane after me.

Out of enthusiasm for this city, my first book, about Odessa, is written. It is the first German travel guide for this city, and maybe the first such book at all, in recent years. And, after all, I have more than enough to do with the book, if I don't start thinking about the opera. The book turns out beautifully. The first edition is printed in Odessa. We published it directly in two languages, German and also English, in print runs of three thousand copies each. The marketing and sales functioned quite well at this time. Every summer there were many Germans and also English-language visitors in the city. We sold the books to them. We – at the time that was a tour guide, with whom I collaborated, and the *Friends of the Opera*, to whom we donated a portion of the revenues from the sales.

In those days, the opera performances were only mediocre, even though first-class singers were available in Odessa. But, of course, the best emigrated as soon as they had a chance. They earn more abroad! In Ukraine – in Odessa – art is not nearly as highly regarded as is always purported.

Eventually, an evening gala takes place. I want to also attend but I don't have a ticket. My job in Odessa is already over. What should I do? I rely on old contacts and somehow finagle myself in while others just press their noses on the windows and are only allowed in thirty minutes before performance begins. A whole tub full of flowers is carried in, to be later presented by the audience to the singers, dancers, and other artists. That is customary and a habit which I have known since Soviet days. Finally, a narrow door wing opens on each side, for the general public, and the people squeeze, more than walk, through. That is something else which I have known since Soviet days. Don't give the masses too much room; they have to be kept under control. I hunt for a seat, somewhere on the balcony. The deputy director said to do this. He couldn't give me a regular ticket. I meet old acquaintances. It is 7:00 pm. The performance is supposed to begin now. But the curtain doesn't rise until shortly before 7:30. Meanwhile the theater, half-empty only a short time before, has filled. A woman edges her way along the row and takes the seat next to me. I ask her why she is arriving so late. She blames the out-of-town bus, which didn't arrive until 7:00 and then she still had to take a taxi to the theater. She is completely exhausted. I understand. Once again poor organization. It's obvious that the performance can't begin if half of the out-of-town audience members have difficulty arriving on time.

It lies in the nature of my profession. I observe, evaluate, make conclusions, and then write about them. But sometimes I feel as though I have gotten caught in a trap. What seemed disgraceful for a large theater I am now ashamed to admit to myself. Why do I pass judgment on others, whose life and customs and also opportunities in life are something I don't at all know well enough. Should I be ashamed of this? No, certainly not, but I should develop understanding.

In those days, beginning in 2005, it began – marketing for Ukraine, first with the job as consultant for culture and tourism then, in more depth, my personal marketing for a country that had become dear to my heart. I write two more books, one about Ukraine in general and the other about Lemberg, *Lviv* in Ukrainian. But before this I am still in Odessa. Meanwhile I have turned fifty. The ties are becoming tighter. In particular, I have purchased an apartment, one more tie to this country. It is in the ulitsa Pushkinskaya. I deliberately write that in the Russian version. In Ukrainian the street is called vulytsya Pushkinska. The difference is not great but in Odessa more Russian is spoken than Ukrainian. I rush through the renovation, taking only six weeks. Friends and acquaintances are surprised by the speed. For me that's normal. In Germany it would surely have taken only half the time. Of course, I pester the workers daily, I supervise everything myself, and once again I know everything better.

My job leaves me enough freedom for the renovation. Thank heavens. That is the positive side of this work. The negative side is the constant stress in this country. Everything is always different. It's not enough that I have to pay every little bill for telephone, gas, and electricity in cash – which involves a lot of legwork because I have to appear everywhere personally. In addition, again and again something unforeseen happens. In one of the major examples of this, construction begins on the lot adjacent to the building my apartment is in. When digging the hole for the construction, the sides were not properly shored up. My apartment develops one giant crack and many small ones. I am in Germany when I receive the news in

December. What should I do? Naturally, I buy a ticket immediately and fly to Odessa to see for myself what has happened there. I am shocked, distraught, and bewildered, when I see it. It's no use talking to the construction firm. They refuse to accepts the costs for a proper renovation of my new apartment. I hire a lawyer, the best in Odessa, who is one of my friends today. She successfully fights in court for me and within four years wins an impressive sum which allows me to renovate the apartment and then later sell it for a good price. But how aggravating, how stressful!

That's all my own fault, because I just didn't want to let go. I did want to turn my back on the country, several times. Why is that so difficult?

My beautiful apartment in Odessa – the living room …

… and the sunny kitchen

The amazing balcony …

… for relaxing moments

Shooting practice

My greatest self-experiment

Each meter toward the west, each additional minute of flying time, makes me feel better. I am flying toward the sunset and it seems to me that I am flying toward the sunrise. Especially when I board a Lufthansa plane; I already feel at home – so nice and German. The tension begins to fall away, and not only because of the two small bottles of champagne that I enjoy this time, in business class. The West – a simpler life? But at the same time I read in the business section of one of the leading German business newspapers about Germany's slowness in asserting itself in international markets. Is German workmanship so bogged down? Yes, each system that becomes entrenched in itself begins to be sluggish and lazy.

It is difficult to accept the responsibility that life demands every day. For Ukrainians, responsibility is a foreign word. No one accepts responsibility and doesn't even know what it really is – perhaps only has an inkling. I am already too exhausted to even think about it any more; about what and how I can write about this country and about the morass in which it finds itself. Everything seems so hopeless. A person is the way he is or the way he was raised to be. It's so easy to only hear or only do whatever seems pleasant. And then to simply say that the telephone wasn't working or something else wasn't functioning. If I were asked to write about Ukraine again today, all I would have to do was get out the articles that I wrote more than twenty years ago, change the names, then publish them. Most of what I wrote then still applies today.

My stays in Ukraine were the greatest self-experiment of my life, aside from life itself and my spiritual plan. Twenty-five years of personal borderline experiences; twenty-five years of scarcity versus abundance; twenty-five years of political doctrine versus freedom; twenty-five years of contradictions, love, problems, solutions, reports, and attempts to explain the Ukrainian world or the Ukrainian part of the Slavic world. Occasionally I dreamt that the Russians would come and occupy the city hall of Weilheim and I would be called on to help, with my language abilities.

Twenty-five years long I was also running away from myself. For twenty-five years I labored outside of myself and "plowed" the field of East Europe/Ukraine. I failed at the attempt and grew with the attempt. I failed because I can't change a country and its people – no matter how many consulting contracts I receive and fulfill, no matter how many chances I have to "instruct" or "convert" the people. It's impossible. I grew because along the way I found the way to myself, more and more, and this process is still continuing.

I did everything that I could to not have to leave Ukraine. At the beginning and at the end I almost even became a Ukrainian bride; almost married a young Ukrainian from my first seminar group in order to get unlimited residence permits – for Germany for him and for Ukraine for me.

In the course of the twenty-five years, I left the church and joined the church. Ukraine – twenty-five atheistic years? Every seven years, something in your life changes, commented Pastor Hadem in Weilheim, when I signed the application to rejoin the Lutheran church on March 15, 2013. Every seven years the body regenerates itself said my dear, old, long-time friend Carl. And my girlfriend Beate once said that my work in Ukraine seemed to be something like my personal pilgrimage on the Way of Saint James. Perhaps. If that is really the case, then there should also be a goal, shouldn't there be? Whoever goes on a pilgrimage is searching for something – a treasure, himself, something very personal or spiritual – is in the process of dealing with something, or trying to let go of something ….

Perhaps without really seeking it, I encountered my own pilgrimage. I wandered through Kiev, through the Carpathian mountains, with a ship along the Dnipro, over hill and dale, through Odessa, drove around the Crimean peninsula, through Kharkiv and Donetsk, through the political morass, through an obscure economy, on many different paths. On my pilgrimage I suffered, was happy, celebrated, loved, loathed the stones in my path and, when possible, moved them out of the way. I also collected them, like trophies, and contemplated them. And I found a treasure – one that I hadn't necessarily been searching for, one that I simply encountered. It is very deep inside myself. I found myself and the treasure inside myself.

On March 24, 2013, I publicly demonstrated becoming a member of the Lutheran church with a communion in Weilheim i.OB (in Upper Bavaria) – with conviction for myself, for the belief, for my family, for a fundamental trust. I feel it now.

And sometimes I dream that I meet Sergey again. Perhaps as an old woman. We meet somewhere, look at one another, and … understand one another, without any words.

Kiev, in the early Nineties, not far from my apartment…

… runs the tram

Independence Square (Maidan) 2014 – commemoration of the dead

I try on a Ukrainian wreath ornament with flowers

The Euromaidan

And then the so-called "Euromaidan"* began, the public protests against the government (2013). I hadn't expected that. I only know them as patient individuals with a fatalistic "Oh, we can't change anything anyway" attitude. But now the Ukrainian people were striking out, to become really independent, free from power struggles, corruption, and oppression. Now they are fighting for their own human values. I sympathize. I know the place and the shopping street, Khreshchatyk, on which I once danced. I see the photos of the crowds of people on Independence Square (Maidan). Day and night they stand there, and they have been standing there for a month now. Soup kitchens, tents, slogans, concerts, speeches. The opposition is organized around the "UDAR" party of the former world-champion boxer, Vitali Klitschko. I follow the developments and speak to people, to my friends, and try to visualize what is happening there, in "my" beloved Ukraine. I am left out because I am sitting comfortably in Germany. And I am suffering from the fact that I am not there.

For more than twenty years I have been campaigning for the recognition of Ukraine as a country in its own right and not just as the much-evoked political buffer zone between East and West Europe. In particular I want others to become acquainted with the people

---

* Maidan means square in Ukrainian language

who live there. Finally, people are watching Kiev. But it is different than it was before, different than the Orange Revolution in 2004. Now things are serious. I can feel it. But unfortunately I am lacking the right perspective of Ukraine – as I can see from my position on the outside. Can an opposition comprising three very different persons and their followers really take a stand and initiate a new era in Ukraine? Isn't the opposition, made up of the former boxer, Vitali Klitschko, and the two hitherto little-noticed young politicians, Oleh Tyahnybok and Arseniy Yatsenyuk, much too inexperienced? Which role is being played in the background by Petro Poroshenko? And: Is someone in Europe possibly pulling the strings of these demonstrations? Does Europe want to have Ukraine for itself and skid into a new Cold War with Russia? Was the Cold War ever really over? Sure, I also think about the role Russia is playing; somehow I have become "Ukrainified" by spending such a long time in this country. Recently I met some Russians and at first I eyed them critically, as some Ukrainians also do, until I realized that they were also very friendly, well-educated, good people. And they also told me that when they met Ukrainians, then they were also regarded with a wait-and-see attitude. There are new divisions between people who are neighbors and in some cases even relatives. Is this the doing of West Europe? Or does it come from even further west? The fact is that both Russia and Ukraine are among Germany's immediate neighbors. With both countries we have written history in different ways. People of both countries look to us to find standards and values for their own lives. And we can also learn something from them. But to do this, we must be open. The people of Ukraine are now standing up for themselves. No one is really honestly supporting them. Europa claims to want them as a part of Europe, but without having to invest too much work. Russia also wants them. After all, Ukraine has its black earth and much more which is worth owning.

It is Christmas. I am invited to one of the ARD's broadcasters, for a studio discussion. For days I ponder what I should say, how I should say it, how I can explain the situation in Ukraine. Suddenly, on the day on which the discussion is to take place, I receive a phone call, "We have to postpone it." The former Russian industrial tycoon, Mikhail Khodorkovsky, has been released. Vladimir Putin, Russia's powerful president, has pardoned him. Khodorkovsky has flown to Berlin and from there is calling the tune with the media, despite the fact that he also earned billions of dollars as a young man, just like the son of Ukrainian President Yanukovych, against whom people in Kiev are demonstrating. It's clear that the Russian man, who has just been released from prison, is important, but once again Ukraine finds itself playing a minor role. Apparently (German) media prefer to jump on an existing bandwagon rather than building a new one. I am disappointed and sad. Admittedly, I am assured that I can look forward to a new interview date, one week later. But how much can happen in Ukraine in the meantime? After all, this is all about a nation with approximately 46 million people.

These people are not split, as is often claimed. In the east as well as in the west of Ukraine, in the south and also in the north, they are all people and they consider themselves Ukrainian. Of course, it is true that those in the south and the east fear that they could be forbidden to speak Russian and only be allowed to speak Ukrainian. Others fear that the European Union could interfere where it is not wanted. After all, they know Russia better; it is (almost) like family. But even these critics are people who wish for a good life, a life in which it is possible to make plans, in which it is possible to adhere to values, as one imagines the case in Europe to be.

I offer my services to numerous media. Some of the reports of my colleagues leave me disappointed and angry. Too little background information; too little real knowledge about what is happening on Maidan at that moment. Members of all groups are standing there – opponents of the regime and also those who claim to be supporters of the regime are demonstrating. When the supporters have fulfilled their "paid service", they change over to the regime opponents. That's what insiders tell me. And they are all Ukrainians or people who live in Ukraine.

Several years ago I functioned as an election observer for the Organization for Security and Co-operation in Europe (OSCE). All night long a colleague and I followed on the heels of the Ukrainians, to observe the counting of the votes. We argued with the Ukrainians, discussed with them, and tried to obtain access to "secret" rooms. It was a real tug of war over control or the hindrance of it. Unexpectedly, in the middle of the night, more boxes of ballots were delivered, which ostensibly were to be counted. Tellingly there was no light; power failure – or whatever – was given as the reason. In the dim light of a lantern the boxes were unloaded and we two were prevented from getting a look. As the time approached 5:30 am, and the whole hassle was over, the table was pragmatically set for breakfast, and as always for special occasions, of course with vodka, bacon, and all sorts of delicacies. The plates were crowded closely together. We, the election observers, found ourselves surrounded by the election workers, who we had been previously supposed to monitor. At first, I didn't want to even sit down at the table. But there they were again, the people, the Ukrainians. They had cast off their official function and were amiably raising their glasses to me.

Suddenly I receive a phone call. I am asked for an article about the world boxing champion and candidate for the office of president of Ukraine, Vitali Klitschko. Later he withdrew his candidacy in order to support the candidacy of Petro Poroshenko. In May 2014

Klitschko then became mayor of Kiev. The article is to be written in a casual style, for a magazine. But how can I write casually when the situation is so serious? I am supposed to describe how popular Klitschko is in Ukraine and how he is depicted in Germany and the German media. I am even offered a trip to Kiev. "Sure, fly there – right away, today or tomorrow." I am taken aback, surprised, and can't make up my mind. I ask friends in Kiev how the situation is and what might happen. For me, things are happening too fast, although I am usually spontaneous and have always wanted to take a short trip to Kiev, on the spur of the moment. And now … what is it that I am feeling? I am simply afraid. Afraid for the first time since I have been traveling to Ukraine. What can happen? Will I get safely through the border control at the airport? Will I get back home safely? Do I dare to go to the Maidan? "Better not," advise friends via e-mail and Skype. It is indeed dangerous there. In particular, people of the press are being attacked; are being shot at, below the belt, with rubber bullets. The people in uniform, whoever they might be, don't stop at journalists, foreign or native.

At the same time, outside the Maidan, life in Kiev is taking its totally normal course, as always. But as soon as people come home, they immediately turn their television on, to follow what is happening. Everything revolves around a few questions: When will President Yanukovych be defeated? When will he resign? When will there be new elections?

I am completely shaken and upset and don't understand what is happening there. So I do have to open a new chapter after all.

On route in East Ukraine with the OSCE

Mission with the OSCE

It has to be. At home in Germany, I only sit at my computer anyway, following the latest pieces of news. So why not just signal to the Organization for Security and Co-operation in Europe (OSCE) that I am ready to go to Ukraine as an observer, as a monitoring officer, and see with my own eyes what is happening there? After all, the task of observing a situation and reporting about it to the organization, which in turn informs the global public, is exactly in accordance with my profession as a journalist. That's what I learned how to do. That's what I can do. So, back again to the country which I thought I had left for good, except for my still-existent apartment in Odessa. Obviously, with my professional background, I was accepted immediately. My deployment station was Kharkiv, in East Ukraine. I didn't want to go there at all; I wanted to go to Odessa. But all the pleas and interventions were no help. I had to go and, in the end, I was also satisfied with the assignment. Kharkiv is beautiful; a wonderful city with large squares, wide streets, huge parks. After all, it was the former capital of Ukraine, before Kiev was declared to be the political center in 1934. And I was very happy there. I spent more than eight months in Kharkiv. Together with my colleagues, we drove through the surrounding area, patrolled in the city, and met with people – the mayor, county commissioners, police, and many others – to repeatedly ask the same questions, as mandated by the OSCE: how the security situation was; what these people had observed; how they were dealing with the many internal refugees; whether or not paramilitary groups or non-governmental agencies (NGOs) were involved in the conflict; and other similar questions. It was depressing for me to be in Ukraine, this time for entirely different reasons than had previously been the case. The armed conflict between pro-Russians and pro-Ukrainians in East Ukraine is very serious. All dialog partners repeatedly emphasized how much they hoped that everything would finally stop. No one understood it and no one understands it. It is not primarily a conflict between Russians and Ukrainians. So many of them are even related to one another, and that not only in eastern Ukraine. But there, in particular, busloads of Russians used to arrive, for example to shop and refuel in Kharkiv because it was less expensive for them there. Afterwards they went to restaurants to celebrate and sing Ukrainian songs. Just a normal neighborhood conflict? No. I had more the feeling that a kind of virus was spreading there, like an infection which was brought to Ukraine from the outside. I never understood the details, nor the procedure of the OSCE and the politicians who arrived from abroad, for negotiations. I often asked myself: What do they want to talk about? Do they know Ukraine? Have they ever lain on Ukrainian soil and inhaled the scent of Ukrainian nature – or swum in the Dnipro or in the Black Sea? Have they ever stood in the shoes of a Ukrainian? Or those of a Russian? In my eyes, a political visit offers little chance for a true converging.

I worked for the OSCE for sixteen months and still remained in the dark, without knowing or understanding what was really happening there, what the trouble was in Ukraine. For me, the expert on Ukraine, that was disconcerting and often even frustrating. I listened to the people who told me what connected them to Russia. I talked to fathers who had one son in the army on the Russian side, and the other, on the Ukrainian side. One such father simply feared that one day the two sons might confront one another. I follow the coverage in the German media and am dismayed by so much ignorance or prejudices and the eternal blather in the talk shows, with moderators who also don't know the country or the people. It all makes me dreadfully sorry. I can't go on any longer. It is too much war for me. And I can't do anything. Just watch as Ukraine gradually gets dismantled. I can't endure it. Moreover, I am bound to a mandate. I can't decide freely with whom and how long I talk about which topic or who I visit, as I used to do. That's too restricted for me. I am suffering. I quit – reluctantly, to be sure. Am I betraying Ukraine if I no longer work for the OSCE? Have I betrayed my own plan for peace? I go with a heavy heart, but at the same time also with a light step because now I have another destination: California. I must go there. My former English teacher comes from there. I met him in 2014, in the language school in Kharkiv, in East Ukraine. He impressed me with his lifestyle – only one pair of shoes, living at the simplest level, and always still sharing whatever he had. I thought that it was his voice I was following, when he returned to his home in California for a couple of months because he needed a break from Ukraine. I buy a ticket to San Francisco. But first I still really have to tie off my loose ends in Ukraine. That means selling my apartment in Odessa, getting rid of my household goods, and really and truly saying good-bye. That means a lot of work is still necessary. It takes several months. But suddenly everything seems so easy. Why? Don't I owe Ukraine anything more? At my last OSCE station, in Dnipropetrovsk, I was again constantly impressed. In the first place, I had a beautiful apartment and, secondly, very nice landlords and also a nice neighbor – immediately like family. Is that only the case because they are Ukrainians? But I want to leave. I have to leave. Now it's time for something else. No longer too much engagement. But still ... Once again there is a Taxi driver with whom I become friends – like in Kiev or Kharkiv or Odessa – again there are people, again relationships grow. No, wait. I want to leave. I have to leave.

Then the time has come. There are buyers for my apartment in Odessa. My lawyer takes care of everything for me, with a power of attorney, while I sit in the OSCE office in Dnipropetrovsk and go on patrol from there. Then, finally, I have resigned. The last days in Ukraine have begun. Simultaneously, I receive an invitation to appear on television, as a discussion partner in the *Planet Wissen* program of the Westdeutscher Rundfunk (WDR, national television of western Germany), to give my view of the situation in Ukraine. The WDR even sends a cameraman to Odessa, to film my leaving; the editor also comes along, because of personal interest. I drive through the city once more in the bright yellow convertible of one of my friends. The going-away party in my apartment is wonderful. Everyone comes once more, all my friends: Anna, Galya, Tanya, Igor, Misha, Anya, the other Misha and his wife and child. I spend all day preparing food. This time the table has to be really full once more: appetizers, salmon, olives, bell peppers – peeled especially by Anna – a huge cake, and in the oven, a curried fish goulash with vegetables, and

Farewell drive with the convertible

added to all of that green salad, fruit salad, a cheese platter, red wine, white wine. The weather on this last day of August is beautiful. My balcony gets lots of use. Once again I push the grape vine up and tie it back, so that it doesn't bother the guests. I am given gifts. How in the world am I going to get them all to Germany? We sing and laugh, and cry. Yes, that's part of it also. I am moved. The party and the film of the WDR are wonderful gifts for me, as a conclusion and as a souvenir. Of course, I am also sad after so many years. More than a quarter of a century have come together there in Ukraine. I cry and I laugh; and I laugh and I cry. The parting is now getting seriously near. When I clean out the cupboards and shelves in my apartment, the melancholy keeps surfacing. How wonderful it all was – the long summer evenings on my large balcony, with friends and a bottle of red wine; the long walks by the sea; the wonderful opera; the surroundings with the black soil and huge fields of wheat and sunflowers. Everything which has grown dear to my heart must now be let go of. But there is no other choice. I have to go to California. My inner voice is calling ….

And, after all, there is war in Ukraine, a war that I can't prevent.

I learn to play the Russian bajan …

Everyone in Ukrainian national costume

… and wear a helmet and protective vest

Stop-off in Kiev – Podol neighborhood

The last sip of vodka

I'm sad. What happened to "my" Ukraine? Once again I am observing from a distance the things that are happening there. And this makes my heart ache. My eyes are caught by the bottle which I brought from Kiev years ago. It is still standing there, in my kitchen. Meanwhile Sasha is in the USA, as are his wife Zina, and the children and grandchildren. The bottle has stayed with me. A little bit is left in the bottle. Is it from the original contents or has it been refilled? It doesn't matter. The vodka is the same. The most important thing is the bottle itself. I received it on one of my birthdays from Sasha and Zina. The label says the following in Russian:

Изготовления в Украине
для очаровательной женщины
семейным дуэтом
Саши и Зины Чернышевичей,
с пожнланиями добра,
здоровья, счастья и удачи!

Пусть водка нашей Украины
тебя согреет в трудный час.
Налей сто грамм от Саши, Зины
И вспоминай почаще нас!
КИЕВ 2002

The translation is:
Made in Ukraine
for a charming woman
by the family duett
Sasha and Zina Chernychevich;
wishing you all the best,
and great health, happiness, and success!

May the vodka of our Ukraine
warm you in difficult times.
Pour yourself one hundred grams from Sasha and Zina
and remember us often!
KIEV 2002

Now we have the year 2015. I open the bottle. It's time for that sip of vodka – the vodka from Zina and Sasha, a symbol of their love, their good will, their friendship – thirteen and a half years after I received the gift. I pour some in a glass. This time I have to do it myself. After all, Sasha is in America. The scent of the vodka brings back old memories. How it was back then, how we celebrated, how happy we were. Today we are older. The mood is different. We have changed, and progressed. The friendship has not abated. Our entire common past is contained in this scent of vodka, which has been mixed with paprika and honey. I put the glass to my lips. The liquid in the glass is golden yellow, like the fields of sunflowers in Ukraine at the end of summer. Sasha, pour one more! I am drinking this last swallow with you, to you, and to us all. Then there will be no more Ukraine in my life – only the friends. Maybe they will come visit me, if I emigrate to California. I love you all, unconditionally. You are what makes Ukraine special. You are life and love. I have lived with you and through you. I always felt that I was in good hands. Thank you! The bottle is not yet quite empty.

In a few days I will travel to San Francisco for the second time. I am expected there, not only by my dear friend Trevor, whom I met via the "bridge" of Ukraine (on a roundabout route), but also by Lena, Aleksander, and the dog. Lena is related to Sasha and Zina. Sasha is her uncle. I had simply asked Sasha if he knew anyone in San Francisco. Yes, he knew Lena. And now I am a guest there, again in a little part of Ukraine. Won't it ever let go of me … or I it? Inevitably I compare America – California – with Ukraine. Some things remind me of Ukraine. On my travels through the vastness of California I sometimes see rusted cars and water tanks, untidy farms, etc. just like in Ukraine. And it seems to me that there is more freedom than in Germany, a more relaxed attitude.
Somewhere during my trip through California I read a text. One line of the text impressed me:

"The imperishable gold of spiritual identity."

That sounds so good and comforting. Yes, that which we experience on the inside also appears on the outside. Originally I went to San Francisco because of my Californian English teacher. But then I met Trevor in San Francisco, in the meditation group of the Self-Realization Fellowship which was founded by Paramahansa Yogananda. It is wonderful. And I can only keep repeating:

Thank you, Ukraine, for everything with which you have prepared my path thus far; for how well meaning you were with me; for how well you received me when I was searching, when I wanted to give, but didn't know what. Thank you, Ukraine, for the many opportunities to hone myself on you, always thinking that I was working for you and your people. Thank you for pushing me out of the nest when I was fully fledged. Thank you for always remaining true to me, never leaving me, and helping me again and again. Thank you Ukraine for the eternal love.

The last sip of vodka – it will remain in the bottle, in case of emergency. As long as some vodka remains, I can always say:

"Sasha, pour one more!"

Thank you

Ukraine – thank you.

Thank you Svetlana, Grisha, Sergey, Sasha, Zina, Inna, Dima, Edik, Gosha, Yura, Georgiy, Anna, Ivan, Vasya, Lena, Tamara, Anya, Juppes, Dieter, Ella, Rainer, Lisa, Erich, Lolita, Bernd, Carl, Karin, Beate, Michael, …
……

Thank you to my parents, who helped me and let me become the person that I am today. Thank you, universe. Thank you, God. Thank you, Jesus, thank you Mary, and all the saints.

Thank you to my entire extended family.

Thank you Herbert and Brigitte, Benedikta and Dietmar who helped me find this path.

Thank you to Karl-Heinz for the patient editing of my books.

Thank you to more than twenty-five difficult, wonderful years in Ukraine, with Ukrainian people who have become my friends. Years which were shaped by suffering, love, and many other human emotions. Years full of incomprehension, misunderstandings, stupidities, stories, and again and again love, love …

Thank you, Trevor, for catching me after so many turbulent years in a sea of friendship, love, and warmth!

More books by

Brigitte Schulze is a cosmopolitan with close ties to her home country, who loves contrasts. Wherever she lives, she likes to take a closer look and write things down. This is how her books came about. Out of the curiosity about and the interest in her surroundings and the people – in Ukraine as well as in Germany.

Ukraine … as I love it. Come along with me!

(German text) An unusually personal and practical travel compendium with ten tour routes and many encounters with people. Presented on 324 pages, with profound background knowledge. One chapter is dedicated to the Crimean Peninsula, before it was annexed by Russia. It is not only the approximately 300 color photos and 20 map segments, the tips, and clearly displayed information boxes which still make this book an important companion on a trip to Ukraine but, above all, the chapters about the mentality and people who live there that give the reader a real feel for the country – and one which is not diminished by the year of publication, 2010.
ISBN 978-3-9810467-3-1, € 24.80

Brigitte Schulze

Odessa ... as sparkling as Champagne. Feel the tingle!

(German text) The humor of the people in Odessa can be experienced in this book. The exuberant city has a unique pulse. The internationality and joie de vivre of its population are legendary. In Odessa, daily life and theater, reality and illusion merge wonderfully. The city is a "special case", as the author writes in the opening chapter. For ten years, she lived and worked in Odessa. The Black Sea is as much of an attraction, as are the wonderful buildings of the international architects who were active here, in particular the great opera house. Of course, the war in East Ukraine has also left its mark on Odessa. The people have become more pensive. And they are searching for their identity as Ukrainians, even though many of them are Russian or identify with Russia. This wonderful book contains lots of insider information, more than 250 color photos, and map segments. The book was first published in 2013 and will remain relevant for much time to come.
ISBN 978-3-9814225-4-2, € 18.95

**Garmisch-Partenkirchen
Edgy and authentic.
Discover why!**

(German text) Garmisch-Partenkirchen is a world-famous, charming market town in Germany's Werdenfelser Land. Two towns have become a brand name. Partenkirchen is older than Garmisch. The double identity in the daily life of the two towns can definitely be seen as an advantage. Much comes in twin packs – clubs, fire departments, festivals, traditions …. take a look for yourself! As is the case with all other books written by the author, this one is written in a very personal style. She described the two old towns, Partenkirchen and Garmisch, and what they have become since the forced merging in 1935: a ski resort of Olympic importance, a renowned German vacation destination, and a health spa famed for its good climate, traditional and cosmopolitan, in which an international public plays and enjoys themselves. A local book seller inspired the author and felt that this book just had to be written.

244 pages with approx. 300 color photos and map segments. Published 2016.

ISBN 978-3-9814225-7-3, € 18.99

Lemberg … simply delightful. Give it a try!

(German text) With this book you will easily find your way through Lemberg's streets and lanes and enjoy the spirit of this old city, declared a World Heritage Site by UNESCO. Its politically turbulent past is immediately visible in its architecture. And the cake is absolutely delicious! By the way, Lemberg is only approximately 80 kilometers from the Polish border. 204 pages 200 color photos and map segments. Published 2012.
ISBN 978-3-9810467-4-8, € 16.80

Weiheim i.OB … the Holy Ghost comes later. Activate it!

(German text) The site of an ancient cultural heritage, charming, old, dreamy, historical, tolerant, colorful, Bavarian, versatile, traditional, vivacious, musical. Here people live and let live. An enchanting bedroom community, and not only for the author! 236 pages, 250 color photos and map segments. Published 2013.
ISBN 978-3-9814225-6-6, € 18.95

pili edition

pili edition has its roots in the German publishing house, *Brigitte Schulze Verlag*. Subjects and themes of both publishing houses are inspired by the author, Brigitte Schulze Pilibosian. Her life was wonderfully divided between Germany and Eastern Europe and finally took her to the United States of America, to California. The miracle of meeting her husband in San Francisco and starting a new chapter in her life happened on her way to discovering her heart and letting her heart guide her way. Follow us ...

www.pili-edition.com

www.ingramcontent.com/pod-product-compliance
Lightning Source LLC
Chambersburg PA
CBHW021129300426
44113CB00006B/345